No Perfect Parent Just a Perfect Purpose

Keys to Unlocking Every Child's Greatness

TONYA MILLIGAN

PUBLISHED BY FIDELI PUBLISHING, INC.

No Perfect Parent
Just a Perfect Purpose

Keys to Unlocking Every Child's Greatness

© 2019 by Tonya Milligan

All rights reserved.

No portion of this book may be reproduced, stored in a retrieval system, or transmitted in any form or by means of electronic, mechanical, photocopy, recording, scanning, or another excerpt for brief quotations in critical reviews or articles, without the prior written permission of the publisher.

ISBN: 978-1-948638-30-2 (paperback)

Unless otherwise indicated, all Scripture quotations are taken from the King James Version of the Bible.

Published by

Fideli Publishing, Inc.
119 W. Morgan St.
Martinsville, IN 46151

www.FideliPublishing.com

Dedication

This book is dedicated to the man of my dreams—for always loving me, blessing me with all of his might, and never giving up.

My husband is an incredible dad; he follows God and has never succumbed to the struggles that he has faced in his life.

Acknowledgements

Thank you so much to my mom and dad. My soul rejoices that God choose you to be my parents and that you gave me the best-ever brother and sister. I thank my children for being my heartwarming blessings that never stop giving. I would like to give a standing ovation to all who helped with the last chapter, sharing their words of wisdom, thoughtful insight, and life experiences. Last but not least, thank you family and friends—your support and prayers have been my wings.

Table of Contents

Acknowledgments .... *v*

Forward by Mary Morgan .... *ix*

Chapter One	Are You Planning to Fail?	1
Chapter Two	He is in Control	13
Chapter Three	Revealing Greatness Isn't Easy	33
Chapter Four	Get Help!	61
Chapter Five	NITRO = Explosive Love	73
Chapter Six	Embrace the Power of Play	95
Chapter Seven	Ducks, Eagles, and Naysayers	115
Chapter Eight	The Secret Gift	135
Chapter Nine	Speak Life	149
Chapter Ten	How Long is the Season?	161
Chapter Eleven	107 Perspectives	173

Foreword

Tonya and I met by chance. It was the spring of 2017 and we found ourselves seated next to each other at my first Christian Women's Business Organization event. I bet we couldn't have been more than a few moments into our "get-to-know-you small talk" before I said to myself, "This woman gets it."

See, I'm a licensed play and family therapist. I've been in practice for over 40 years. My life has been dedicated to helping families. I specialize in teaching children to connect and form secure relationships with adults, themselves, and their worlds through the power of play. In the process, I also help parents learn more about—and connect with—their children.

So, when Tonya mentioned what she does for work and why, I knew I'd found a kindred spirit. A sister in soul, if you will. Which is why I immediately said "yes!" when she approached me to write the foreword for her book.

As I said, Tonya gets it. She's a woman who, like me, has dedicated her life to helping families. While we may have gone about our mutual mission in different ways—she spent 26 years as an educator and then took what she learned in the classroom and applied it to folks of all ages—our goals have always been the same:

- Help people.
- Help families.
- Help people create healthier families and relationships.

That's why I was delighted and honored when Tonya asked me to be a part of *No Perfect Parent, Just A Perfect Purpose*. The book you are holding is going to teach you to be a better parent and even grandparent. That's what it's about and that's what you can expect to find and learn inside these pages.

Get ready.

Get excited.

Because there are so many useful tools in this book, you'll be amazed. Drawing on her total life experience as a mother, grandmother, teacher, and woman of faith, Tonya has put together a marvelous collection of practical wisdom and inspiration. And it's usable.

The best part of *No Perfect Parent, Just A Perfect Purpose* is the way Tonya writes. She doesn't preach, she teaches. At no point does it feel like she's on a soapbox looking down and scolding you. Instead, it's as if Tonya gently takes your hand, pats it a couple times, and says, "It's okay, I understand. We're in this together and I can help."

I know it might sound cheesy and maybe too good to be true, but this book is for everyone. No matter who you are, you will find something of value in this book to apply to your life and improve your relationships. While it's true that Tonya uses the parent-child relationship to illustrate her points, the principles she teaches are universal.

Whatever has happened in your life that has brought you here, holding this book, trust that you are in the right place. If you have come to this book full of frustration, overwhelmed, and feeling like you're drowning in all the responsibilities of parenting, this book will help. If you're sad, concerned, and despairing about your current relationship with your child—or anyone for that matter—know, too, that this book will help.

Inside these pages, Tonya makes the difficult or even impossible seem easy and attainable. She takes concepts that are simple to talk about, like, "Allow yourself to love like you've never been hurt," "Overlook the things that offend you," and "Make a schedule for your child," and breaks them down into manageable, doable steps.

No Perfect Parent, Just A Perfect Purpose is full of acronyms and quotes. I'd like to share a few that I've found myself constantly coming back to after I finished reading Tonya's book. The first is NITRO. It stands for:

Never give up on love
Interrupt negative thought patterns with positive ones
Trust God
Reconciliation is always the goal
Overlook offenses.

It's a concept I've found myself putting into practice from the moment Tonya taught it to me.

There are also two quotes that resonated deeply with me as soon as I read them. In fact, I've already put both of them up on the wall in the play center I run.

"It's easier to raise strong children than it is to repair broken men."
— Fredrick Douglas

*"Children are not a distraction from important work.
They are the most important work."*
— C.S. Lewis

As I said before, I'm excited—for you, for the journey you're about to take, and for all the wonderful power-thoughts and messages you're about to learn. I'm also excited for Tonya. Writing a book is no small feat, trust me, I know! But to have written a good book that legitimately helps people become better parents and humans, that's something else altogether.

Please enjoy, and trust God that you are right where you're supposed to be, getting the help and inspiration you need. After all, who else (but God?) do you think arranged for Tonya and me to accidentally meet that spring day a couple years ago?

Mary Morgan
Licensed Marriage and Family Therapist &
Registered Play Therapist, Author, *The Treasure of Toys*

CHAPTER ONE

Are You Planning to Fail?

*Our Children Are a Gift,
and We Want to Give Them Our Best*

> *Behold, children are a heritage from the* LORD,
> *the fruit of the womb is a reward.*
> — Psalms 127:3 (ESV)

Do you have hopes of being a perfect parent or at least of coming close? Or are you a realist who has accepted that it is impossible, so you wonder why one would even try? It is natural to have concerns about what type of parent you will be. Most of us desire to add quality and significance to our children's lives as parents and worry if we will be worthy enough.

But have you ever pondered what God's goal is for you as a parent? If we believe that God is all-knowing, we can't surprise Him. He is aware of our flaws and our frailties. Therefore, parenting merely necessitates that we do the best we can, right? But what does that entail? Our maximum effort is different for each of us. In our attempts to give it our all we should remind ourselves that in our weakness, God's power is always perfect. Consequently, the perfection that we wish to attain as parents is accomplished, just not through us.

Resting in the knowledge that God's perfect plan is achieved offers relief and peace of mind. This peace should be the goal for all parents. It doesn't, however, give us the right to slack off or shun the responsibilities that God has given us as parents. We are obligated as parents of future generations to be accountable and to take our job seriously. The world is full of parenting messages that attempt to instill a leave-it-to-chance attitude in us.

We are all aware that formal training or attending a parenting institution is not a prerequisite for becoming a parent. There is no set of instructions that comes with our child or degree to obtain that prepares us for parenting. How we parent or raise our children is up to each one of us.

Ironically, the law requires us to obtain a license for chauffeuring passengers, providing therapy, and teaching—all services that we provide as parents. Parents do all of these things and more for their children without a license or any pre-conditional professional degree.

Parents make the decision about how much work and training they want to invest into raising their children. We could read parenting books and take a few parenting workshops, but most often, parents improvise. So, let's applaud you now for choosing to do better for your child.

> *We cannot always build the future for our youth,*
> *but we can build our youth for the future.*
> — Franklin D. Roosevelt

> *It is easier to build strong children*
> *than to repair broken men.*
> — Fredrick Douglass

God has given us the order to train our children in the way that they should go, and this is not to be done without deliberation of the consequences, but rather with reverence and intent.

> *Train up a child in the way he should go,*
> *and when he is old he will not depart from it.*
> —Proverbs 22:6 (ESV)

Train (v):
> to teach a person a particular skill or type of behavior through practice and instruction over a period of time.

Understand that there will be days when being a self-focused parent may seem appealing or at least somewhat desirable. There have been days when life was too much for me to do anything but breathe, which definitely left out striving for an Outstanding Mom award. I don't know if this happens to every parent, but I am convinced that exceptional parenting should not be an easy task. It demands hard work, resilience, dedication, and lots of prayers. But anything worth anything has a cost.

Some might refer to a struggling mom or dad as self-centered and non-committed; in short, a bad parent. Let me persuade you that this may not be a correct term for parents who wrestle with putting themselves first in critical situations. Consider that we all fall short of the glory of God at times. Missing the mark happens in many areas of our life, and that includes our parenting skills. We must learn to give ourselves grace as we work to bring greatness to fruition through the lives of our children.

Many parents now are experiencing a trend that may intensify the stress of parenting. It's called social media. It is pervasive and has a strong lure to provoke envy, judgment, and comparison, thus creating insecurities throughout the entire family. Social media stifles the natural tendency of parenthood, which is to meet our children's needs, including some of their desires. Even without social media, parenting is stressful, so limiting your family's exposure to it may be advisable.

This book is not meant to point fingers, judge, or suggest that I have all the answers. This book is meant to embolden parents to remove the guilt and assist them with a vision and a plan for every stage of parenting. I hope that it will encourage you to create a strategic roadmap and be intentional about how you parent at all stages of your children's lives.

I have had parents inquire as to why I am so adamant that they write a formal plan for how they intend to parent. I often want to answer that question with another question. We all see the importance of writing a business plan when contemplating starting a business. And how many of us would hire an architect who refused to submit blueprints for building our house?

Envision a bride deciding to improvise and forego any formal preparation before the matrimonial ceremony. Think no invitations, no dress fittings, no food or cake tasting. She would simply call a few hundred of her closest friends and family members a couple of days prior to the event and ask them to join her and her future husband for a fabulous celebration. With the many details attendant upon hosting a wedding, it would be ridiculous to think that she could accomplish success without a plan.

Doesn't it seem absurd to think of raising our children, who are so much more valuable, without a written plan?

Many of us have heard the quote by Alan Lakin, "*Failing to plan is planning to fail.*" My hope is that this book will help you walk through one of the biggest, most rewarding challenges of your life with the confidence that there is a perfect purpose for you and your child. Greatness is found in our purpose, and we all have purpose. God chose you for your child. Raising your child is your perfect purpose in this season.

You may be wondering what authority I have to write this book. I have more than thirty years of experience in working with children and parents as a teacher and director of childcare programs in schools. I also have strong spiritual discernment, which has allowed me to be a part of thousands of success stories. I am blessed to be the parent of two prosperous adult children and two amazing grandchildren. Yes, spoken just like a grandmother!

I believe that my success with my own children is important for the same reason that a teller at a bank studies real currency rather than counterfeit money. I was a teller for seven years, so I speak with some familiarity in this arena. Recognizing the real thing keeps you from accepting phony imitations.

We have all heard millions of stories about how someone has messed up and learned from their mistakes, which may be true. Nevertheless, the fact is that there are too many ways to blunder parenting to study them all and to devise a successful parenting plan from them. Consider studying the real success stories of those who have navigated the path to achieve victory in parenting.

I love the quote by John C. Maxwell, *"It's said that a wise person learns from his mistakes. A wiser one learns from others' mistakes. But the wisest person of all learns from others' successes."* In short, study the real thing, and you will spot a fake plan for success with ease. Find out what works and how it works best for you.

And, most importantly, God directed me to write this book.

It is time for me to share what I have learned during the last three decades. Presenting some of my triumphs may serve as a template to help you construct your roadmap for intentional parenting.

Yes, I also have stories of life-changing failures as a parent. I learned from them and reminded myself that God would use them too. All parents have times that are not their shining moments and times that they may want to forget.

We know that all things work together for the good of those who love God, who are called according to His purpose.

Romans 8:28 (ESV)

The best part about our failures is that we can learn from them in a profound and individual way that will stay with us forever. We should view our mistakes as lessons designed for our personal growth. Learn from your mistakes, and don't repeat them. And remember that an apology goes a long way toward repairing and healing the hurt caused by our mistakes.

Many times what we perceive as an error or failure is actually a gift. And eventually we find that lessons learned from that discouraging experience prove to be of great worth.
—Richelle E. Goodrich, Author

Learn from every mistake because every experience, encounter, and particularly your mistakes are there to teach you and force you into being more who you are.
— Oprah Winfrey

As a director of a child enrichment program, I learned many valuable life and parenting lessons. I often had the challenging responsibility of telling parents about their child's objectionable behavior, which disrupted the hierarchy of the educational process. Trust me, these were not easy conversations.

Many times I was on the receiving end of a momma bear's wrath or a dad's dismissive nod, an indication that he believed that the behavior simply qualified as boys being boys. God revealed numerous ways to enlighten these parents without offending them.

In fact, in the midst of the process I often became a confidant and sought-out advisor. Parents could tell that I cared about their child and that I was their child's advocate. I have concluded that this was one of the fundamental reasons for my success. Therefore, I hope that you are able to discern my heart as I share with you. Please accept that my goal is to also be your confidant and your child's advocate.

God permitted me to raise two perfect children for His perfect purpose. That's right, they are perfect according to God's plan for their lives. Perfect, not because I say so or because of their own will, but because of the blood that Jesus sacrificed for them.

They are perfect for what they were created to do. It was because of God's guidance that I have children that bless my soul. Sometimes I recognized His hand directing me, sometimes I was oblivious. The entire process helped me raise children that bless our world with their gifts and purpose.

For we are God's handiwork, created in Christ Jesus to do good works, which God prepared in advance for us to do.

Ephesians 2:10 (New International Version)

Let's begin with ten simple principles that God impressed upon my heart to share

1. If it is important, make a plan and get it done.
2. Trust God's sovereignty.
3. Treasures are buried deep and take work to retrieve.
4. We all need help; seek it and receive it.
5. Loving isn't always easy but is always worth it.
6. Everyone needs to play.
7. If God said it, do it! Delay is disobedience.
8. Growth can't happen without pain.
9. Our words may leave lasting scars or add wings to dreams.
10. Find the joy in every season.

These principles are reflected in the coming chapters. Yes, I did refer to these ten principals as being simple, but I meant in nature. I know that as you apply them to your daily life they will require trust, faith, work, and a lot of prayers. Many times I lost focus on these principles and paid dearly with tears and worry. Refocusing isn't always easy, but it is the most effective way to accomplish your goals.

There were many times when I was forced to look within for resilience to encourage myself. Other times God allowed a pastor, my parents, or even my children to set me back on the right track. I have since learned that it is wise to have a mentor or trusted friend to whom you can reach out for support, but only count on God.

I hope that this book will encourage you and help you keep your eyes open for the people that God is using to sustain your focus and calm the distractions. As you go through the chapters please keep a Bible nearby, and stop and pray for clarity and understanding.

CHAPTER TWO

He is in Control

I'd like to tell you a few stories. The events in these stories helped me to realize, without a doubt, that I wasn't calling the shots. Life brought situations that I couldn't control. No matter how much I wanted change or prayed, the outcome wasn't up to me.

I was newly married, 19, and pregnant with my son, Kenneth.

I conceived before I got married. Raised as a Christian, I thought that all eyes looked at me with judgement. Carrying around several bags of guilt doesn't make parenting easier, that is for certain. However, a heart to do the best for my child was the first step in the right direction.

I was six months pregnant when my mother and I started attending a Lamaze course. At a hair over five feet tall, my mom has an infectious laugh and always has an encouraging word for everyone. I chose my mom to assist me with Lamaze, fearing that my new husband wouldn't meet my needs for support. My sister and I are twenty-two months apart, and people often say that we look like twins. She got married in April, I got married one month later in May. She was also pregnant. She and her husband were in the same Lamaze class.

Toward the end of the course the teacher showed what I deemed a disturbing video of a woman giving birth by caesarean section. My sister and I had many conversations about how much anxiety and fear the process of giving birth was generated in us because of watching that video.

Throughout the video I noticed events that troubled me. Two procedures in particular brought forth inconceivable dread, the kind of dread that gives one night sweats. The thought of these things happening to me caused beads of sweat to pop out on my forehead, my hands to shake, and made my stomach feel queasy.

The first disturbing thought was the image of an internal fetal monitor being stuck into the baby's head. I did not want anyone to stick something into my unborn baby's head. Nope, this couldn't happen to my precious baby boy. (A nurse had revealed to me that he was a boy from my previous ultrasounds.)

Second, and undeniably the worst and most feared, was giving birth by caesarean section. My sister and I were horrified and left declaring that we never wanted to go through trauma like what the video showed.

Well, circumstances are not always in our control, and this was the first of many lessons that I would learn in that regard.

I went into labor at 7 a.m. on Friday, December 7, a beautiful, sunny, crisp Colorado morning. Ready and anxious, I had my bag packed with what I thought were the essentials for an overnight stay at the hospital. I called my 20-year-old husband to come home from work at nine that morning.

He picked me up first, and then we swung by for my mom. She had her camera ready, intending to chronicle our new family in a photo book.

"Let's take a picture outside," Mom offered this initial suggestion.

I had gained 28 pounds and couldn't fit into my winter coat. Game nevertheless, I stepped out of the front door and promptly froze in place. I placed one hand on my belly, teeth chattering from nerves and the cold and tried to smile. My husband, noticing my failing attempt to smile, handed me his coat. Mom bundled up like an Eskimo with her scarf and puffy down coat, continued to advise me as to how best to optimize the photographs.

In between contractions, Mom recommended several poses for my husband and me. "Look into each other's eyes, and hold hands."

Posing for pictures added to the exhilaration at first, but when the pain level ratcheted up, it became annoying. Mom has a heart of gold and optimism that touches the sun, so even my short, rude comments didn't faze her.

Rising from a pain-induced crumpled squat, my eyes fixed on Mom, I grumbled, "Can't you see that I'm hurting? Put that camera down right now!"

"You will appreciate this book later, so keep on smiling," Mom chimed in without a change in her ice-cold-lemonade-on-a-hot-summer-day demeanor.

After eighteen hours of labor, my child-birthing process went downhill. My baby was in distress. I had to agree to allow the doctor to insert an internal fetal monitor for the safety of my baby. The nurses took time to reassure me that the monitor had a low risk of causing permanent or long-term complications. They also emphasized the importance of being able to detect how much stress Kenneth was experiencing to prevent jeopardizing his well-being.

After twenty hours of intense labor the doctor declared that it looked as if emergency surgery was imminent. A baby's heart rate should range between 100 and 160 beats per minute. A fetal heart rate that is less than 100 beats per minute is a good indicator that the baby is not receiving enough oxygen. Chances were increasing that my baby would suffer long-term disabilities or—even more devastating—death.

Kenneth's heart rate had dropped dangerously low, to 68 beats per minute.

Twenty-one hours into labor, my doctor entered the room issuing commands to the medical team gathered around me. "Get her to OR eight."

Rushing me down the hall, a nurse holding my IV shrieked, "You need to make a decision about who you want in the OR with you."

The nurse told my mom, my husband, and me that only one support person could go into the operating room with me. Having only seconds to choose, I selected my mother. The nurse pointed my husband toward the waiting area. A cold breeze rushed over me as they swooshed me down the hall. I could see my husband twisting his hat into a tight roll, his eyes glazed over, as he mustered up a slight wave. It was apparent that he would have liked to be the first person informed about the condition of his wife and baby.

While in the operating room my mom witnessed the traumatic birth of her first grandbaby.

The event was so ghastly that even many years later she recalls it with eeriness in her voice. Her clarity and detail is remarkable.

She explains how quickly it became obvious that the birthing process was not going well.

The doctor's eyes widened, and his face lost color. "Get the NICU team in here stat!"

The medical team hastily prepared machines and monitors that beeped, screeched, and had lots of blinking lights. The doctor delivering Kenneth now became more noticeably nervous, wiping the perspiration from his brow with a roll of gauze. His white coat couldn't conceal the rings of sweat forming from under his arms to his waist. The entire medical team sounded anxious as the doctor barked out orders, one right after another without pausing. An intense focus pervaded the room. All faces were solemn as a well-rehearsed team moved in sync.

Due to the urgency of delivering Kenneth, I did not have the choice of being awake for his birth. Someone told me to count from five to one backwards.

"Five, four..." I uttered nothing else.

Mom recalls the doctor cutting into my abdomen as soon as my eyes closed and seeing my open torso looking like a pot of organs.

"Standing next to you I watched as the doctor then made a quick incision into your uterus and pulled Kenneth from the opening. He was the color of the sky on a clear summer day, a perfect baby blue." Mom always tells the story slowly, with a face that fades into outer space, as if she is replaying every detail of a horror movie in her head.

"Dressed in light blue scrubs, the NICU team of five was forcefully rough with his small limp body. Two of the nurses from the team rubbed him frantically from his shoulders to his feet, taking turns when their hands reached exhaustion. His body flopped around, but he didn't make a sound.

"Sarah, a large, stout, brown-skinned nurse with massive hands, thrusted a tube down his throat repeatedly in an attempt to pull the mucous out of his lungs. She muttered 'breathe' each time she pulled the tube out and patted him on the back so hard that it left her hand print.

"All of a sudden, two of the NICU nurses lifted their heads and focused on me. I stood watching with tears welling up in my eyes, shaking and motionless at the same time.

"The eyes of one of the people in scrubs latched onto my eyes and made demands in a raspy voice. 'I need you to wait outside!' I didn't or couldn't move, and no one seemed to have time to follow through on that particular command." Mom always stopped to catch her breath right here.

"I recall a few moments later walking toward the door. I was thinking that when my daughter woke up she would want the details of what happened to her baby boy. I stopped in my tracks, turned back, and carefully took note of every move the doctors and nurses made.

"It was like nothing I had ever seen before. Again, a doctor in a concerned yet stern voice spoke with even more force. 'Wait outside, it will be better for you both.' I wondered if that meant that I was somehow in the way. I moved to a corner of the room. The team fervently worked to help Kenneth breathe on his own, but I couldn't and didn't leave the room. Then, in the next moment, he screamed, and I exhaled in relief. Many of the nurses cheered, and one even clapped. The room seemed to brighten as doctors and nurses sighed with relief. I then realized that Kenneth would be okay."

I appreciated my mom not leaving the room. I missed out on some of the birth, but Mom's vivid and non-wavering recollection of that day is like a video in my mind. That day, the two things that I had known explicitly that I didn't want to be a part of my childbirth experience, happened. Circumstances were truly out of my control. But I thank God—the Master of everything—that He was in control. In the chaos of giving birth, God was in control. Kenneth spent nine days in the Neonatal Intensive Care Unit. I had to leave Kenneth at the hospital, which was an indescribable, gut-wrenching pain. This was just another event that was out of my hands. This hurt so deeply that even my soul wept.

No new mother wants to leave the hospital without her baby, and this 19-year-old mother was overwhelmed with anguish. My baby boy was eventually fine, and I spent a lot of time worrying through that ordeal instead of trusting God.

Kenneth left the hospital on the tenth day, healthy and happy.

Nevertheless, understanding that situations can happen that are out of your control is one thing, living through them is another. It takes courage and perseverance, of which I had a tiny bit of at that time. The good news is that all you need is a little faith.

> *Trust this, faith as small as a mustard seed*
> *can move mountains.*
>
> Matthew 17:20 (NIV)

Walking through a trial that hurts and that you cannot change is scary. You can't predict how things are going to end, but you have to have faith that a power bigger than you will help you through. Remember that fear is the opposite of faith. You must put your faith in a God who avowed, *I will never leave you or forsake you.* Then you must continue to move forward as if on autopilot. Take a single action at a time. Don't overwhelm yourself with trying to look at the *what ifs* or the *shoulds*. Keep things simple. Keep moving and praying.

Try these five STEPS:

1. **S**eek God. Be still before Him and listen.
2. **T**rust the word that God gives you.

   Trust in the LORD with all your heart,
   and lean not on your own understanding.

   Proverbs 3:5 (NIV)

3. **E**quip yourself with God's promises in the area of life that is affected (healing, trust, fear).
4. **P**ray without ceasing. Wake up praying, continue throughout the day, and pray yourself to sleep.
5. **S**tart the process over.

I am confident that this works. These five STEPS have carried me through some dark days. But I trust that this works most of all because God is faithful.

Kenneth weighed more than nine pounds and was similar in size to a two-month-old rather than a newborn when I brought him home. I couldn't even squeeze him into the newborn outfits that I received as gifts for him at the hospital. He had thick, black hair that stood straight up in the air if the blanket rubbed against his head a few times. His skin was whiter than his Caucasian doctor. This was odd because my husband had skin like a milk chocolate bar. Often people thought that his glossy, nickel-sized ebony curls were produced from a chemical process, but they were all natural.

In fact, my baby confused many of the nurses. They tried to give me the Latino baby in the nursery, who was much darker. For me, gazing at Kenneth was pure joy. He could not have been more perfect.

He was a super easy baby. He didn't cry much, and he had a smile that melted my heart. I wanted to hold him all the time, but voices of my family matriarchs resounded in my head. *Don't sit and hold that baby boy all day long, or he will become spoiled.*

I loved Kenneth. I didn't want anyone to call my baby spoiled. I used to lay him down on the bed and snuggle up right next to him with my arm around his infant body. Nothing in my life had ever felt so right. I would do anything for this baby.

Well, at least that is what I wanted to think. As I mentioned, things weren't easy in the delivery process for Kenneth or me. The doctor advised me that I had lost a lot of blood, which caused me to be anemic and cold over the next few months.

I was convinced that if I was this cold, my baby must be freezing. Visiting family members warned me that it was too hot in the house. I disregarded their pleas to turn down the heat. I wrapped Kenneth in layers of blankets. Poor Kenneth was wet with sweat for the first two months of his life.

Kenneth soon became covered with a strawberry red, bumpy rash from his head to his ankles. The doctor counseled me that Kenneth had a severe heat rash and that I was dressing him too warmly. He instructed me not to put blankets on Kenneth while in the house.

I had control over the heat, and I had to exercise control over the feelings that I had myself and turn down the heat. I had to depend on others to tell me how hot it was in the house because my perception was off.

My lesson can be yours. Pray and listen to others when God tells you to. When you have control, use prudence.

I got pregnant a year later with Vance Ryan. At 24 weeks I thought my water broke. I called the doctor and voiced my concern. He told me that the baby most likely kicked my bladder, and he didn't seem troubled. After questioning me about my pain, he suggested that I wait and see if I felt any intense cramping or noticed any bleeding. I called again eight hours later, wanting the doctor to see me. I was not cramping much, but I felt dizzy, nauseated, and my limbs ached. After three panicked phone calls from me, and at my insistence, the doctor finally allowed me to come in.

After I arrived, he did a nitrazine paper swab, a test meant to detect the rupture of the fetal membrane. He maintained that I was mistaken, that my water hadn't broken. He then sent me home. 18 hours later I had a temperature of 102° and was stumbling to maintain my balance. I phoned my mom.

My mother reluctantly decided to drive me to the hospital. My doctor apologized and confirmed that my water had indeed broken and that an infection had spread throughout my body. My baby boy was dead.

The doctor ordered Pitocin to induce labor. Waves of intense labor pains began, and I soon gave birth to a beautiful baby boy, who weighed four pounds, two ounces and was lifeless. He was the color of white bread and had a head full of straight, jet black hair and features much like his older brother, Kenneth.

My spirt shattered, I heard a nurse spew out a series of questions. *"Do you want to have him buried? Can you afford a funeral? Would you like to donate his body to science?"*

I don't recall where my family was. I was 20 years old and distraught. I was clueless about what to do. We didn't have much money, and her questions overwhelmed me.

I'm sure she noticed that I was emotionally devastated, disoriented, and that grief engulfed me. She rubbed my hand and whispered that most mothers allowed the bodies of their babies to be used for science. I moaned, which she took for assent, and she quickly brought a paper to me, which I signed.

Lying there sobbing, I played my life over and over in my head. *All of the things that I have done wrong must have caused my baby to die. Did this happen because of the abortion that I had when I was 17? Is God getting back at me for my sins?*

The abortion itself was painful both mentally and physically. But I felt that surely I had paid for this sin when I hit a seven-year-old girl with my car a few months after the abortion. This event was traumatic for an 18-year-old young woman.

I remembered the pool of blood growing in slow motion around her doll-like head as she lay there, not moving at all. I recalled my screams being the only sound that I could hear, even though emergency vehicles rushed up to the scene with flashing crimson and white lights and sirens blaring. Everything seemed silent compared to my agonized shrieks. In my mind I replayed seeing the petite girl's mother bending over her daughter's lifeless body and moving her mouth, but I couldn't hear anything except my own screams.

The only scriptures that I knew by memory were the Lord's Prayer. *"Our Father, who art in Heaven, hallowed be Thy name. Thy kingdom come, Thy will be done, on earth as it is in heaven. Give us this day our daily bread. And forgive us our trespasses as we forgive those who trespass against us. Lead us not into temptation, but deliver us from evil. For Thine is the kingdom, and the power, and the glory, forever and ever. Amen."*

I remembered shouting this over and over, as I scanned the blocked-off street filling with emergency vehicles. The firetruck was the first to arrive, a couple of marked police cars were next. Then a few unmarked white cars and an ambulance parked all crazy in the middle of a narrow neighborhood street. It was chaos.

In between reciting the Lord's Prayer, I talked to God. I pleaded with Him to not let the girl die.

"She is dead!" I yelled.

One of the firefighters consoled me and stared me straight in the eyes and told me that she wasn't dead. With concern he queried if he could call anyone for me, but it was almost as if he was talking from a mile away. His voice was faint and hard to hear through my ear-piecing cries. A neighborhood lady heard the squealing breaks, the car hitting the girl's body, and the regretful howls that followed. She ran to me, pushing past the fireman.

She took my hand and maneuvered me away from the accident and all the firefighters and the police to her front yard. She was able to pull her telephone outside to the front step because it had a long cord. She handed me the phone, and I called my mom. In the summer of 1982, smart or cordless phones had not been invented, and it wasn't against the law to not wear a seatbelt.

I stopped screaming long enough to try to explain to my mommy what had happened. She tried to console me with the words that she was on her way, and I hung up.

And then I bawled so loudly that my brother covered his ears and whined, "You are hurting my ears." I glanced toward him, realizing that I had forgotten all about him.

I immediately went back to begging God to save the young girl's life. *Please don't let her be dead.*

A policeman approached me in an attempt to interrogate me. He popped off a barrage of questions. "*What happened? How fast were you going? When did you first see the girl?*"

While he spoke, I rocked and whimpered.

I sobbed as I explained. "I had just turned the corner. I was playing around hitting my brakes repeatedly to make my younger brother and his friend, who were not wearing seatbelts, jerk forward. The little girl, riding a big wheel down her driveway, shot out into the middle of the street from between two parked cars. I hit her! Bam! I saw her fly up a bit over my hood and then fall about three feet in front of my car.

"I stepped out of the car and took two or three steps forward, only to see her tiny body curled up on the street and a pool of dark red blood slowly growing around her head."

And that is when the world seemed to close in around me, and I sobbed without restraint.

The policeman tried to reassure me. He told me that it wouldn't have been possible for me to see the girl before she rode into the street. He patted my shoulder and suggested that I try to calm down.

The police investigation concluded that I wasn't at fault. I had been driving at an estimated speed of fifteen miles per hour, and that was deemed as not being a factor in the cause of the accident.

I remember being angry that the girl's mother would let her play in the driveway, where she could ride out into the street. Then I felt an almost irrepressible rage that the young girl picked my car to ride in front of.

So many emotions swirled around in my head, my heart, and my stomach: sadness, anger, and guilt. I was distraught and ashamed that I didn't see the youngster in time to stop my car.

I called the hospital so many times that someone finally took pity on me and disclosed a few details about her condition. The girl had a broken collar bone, a broken pelvis, and her leg was also broken. She likely sustained other injuries as well. I wasn't a family member, so the information was given to me anonymously, but the person informed me that the doctors believed that the girl would recover fully. God was in control.

God saved the little girl, but He didn't save my baby. Why? I didn't realize it at the time, but the tragedy of losing my baby wasn't God trying to hurt me because of my sins. He wasn't trying to pay me back.

But this situation would be used for His glory. Spiritual maturity develops through pain. In fact, through every painful event in my life, God has drawn me closer to Him.

As a teenager, I often verbalized that I didn't like children. After Kenneth was born, I declared, "I only like my child, not other people's kids."

But going home that day without Vance Ryan and grasping the reality that he was gone from this world rendered me forever wounded. The pain is better today, but this event produced in me a profound, heart-felt appreciation and love for every child.

I couldn't explain my excruciating pain back then. I perceived people's comments as callous and cold about my loss. They made remarks like, "*Well, at least you have Kenneth.*" My sister insinuated that I hadn't experienced a loss because it wasn't like I had gotten to know Vance. But she was wrong. I loved him. I had felt the gentle fluttering of his body, I had heard his heart beat. I loved him, I knew him, and my heart was broken.

I suffered through two miscarriages. I also endured two more painful and heartbreaking stillbirths over the next eight years before becoming pregnant with Nicole.

This meant that I was a fanatic about my Kenneth. Some called him my golden child. I wanted to be the best mom that I could be for him. I read parenting books, attended workshops, and asked questions of moms who I respected. If God allowed me to have this blessing, I wanted to do the best that I could for him.

I didn't share my torment with others often, but it was there, growing me into what God planned for me to be, an advocate for children. The events that I considered tragedies were forming the character that I needed to express love more fully as a parent and as an advocate for all children. God was in control, developing the attributes that I needed within me.

Throughout my life God has reminded me numerous times that He is in control. This has been comforting during those times when I felt like I tried my best and nothing seemed to make my situation better.

Know that before your child was even born, God has been preparing you for the moment that you would be called "Mom" or "Dad". Everything that happened in your life before you became a parent has been crafting you for your purpose as the parent of your child. He designated you for the child that He has blessed you with. God doesn't make mistakes, and every one of your life experiences is used as you parent your child.

In Him we were also chosen, having been predestined according to the plan of Him who works out everything in conformity with the purpose of His will, in order that we, who were the first to put our hope in Christ, might be for the praise of His glory.

Ephesians 1:11-12 (NIV)

RECAP

Use STEPS to persevere through challenges:

Seek God
Trust God
Equip yourself with His word
Pray
Start over.

CHAPTER THREE

Revealing Greatness Isn't Easy

Parenting with intention is important in order to allow your child's greatness to shine through. Creating a written plan helps generate positive outcomes. You choose how much detail you want to include. Realize that your plan needs to be flexible. Create a plan along with a schedule to help you implement it. Decide how complex you want your plan to be. You may want to follow the outline of a business plan or use a parenting plan for child custody and customize one of them to fit your family's needs. You can Google either of them for help getting started.

Intentional parenting involves organizing activities at just the right time to be most effective. Optimal success takes into consideration the family habits and moods throughout the day and the week. Try monitoring and charting at what time of day your family functions best. When is your child most relaxed? When does he perform the best? Is it in the morning or the afternoon?

Does your child run out of steam at the end of the week, or does he become more energetic?

Keep in mind that your mental state is just as important to study when creating an ideal schedule. The family is a unit; therefore, you must construct a schedule that works well for every member of your family. Your family schedule is unique and may require some thoughtful deliberation as to how best to structure that schedule.

I think that too often we try to adopt other people's schedules and try to make them fit our life. This likely won't work. Each child and family is different, and the schedules that we devise need to reflect that individuality. In addition, our schedules will change depending upon the season. It is important to evaluate your schedule and make adjustments when needed.

Before you create the schedule, make a productivity chart. This will help your schedule be more effective. Use colored pencils, a notebook, or whatever you generally use to record comprehensive notes. Index cards and a mini file box will also work well.

Use a page or a card for each family member. Write their name on the top of the card. Then write horizontally across the page each hour of the day that this family member is awake, from morning to bedtime. Then, using the numbers one through four from the list below, fill in each hour with one of these numbers for each family member. Do this for one to two weeks. This is what I call a productivity chart.

MONDAY

TIME	7:00	7:30	8:00	8:30	9:00	9:30	10:00	10:30	11:00	11:30	12:00	12:30	1:00	1:30	2:00	2:30	3:00	3:30	4:00	4:30	5:00	5:30	6:00	6:30	7:00	7:30	8:00	8:30	9:00
						AM															PM								
Name 1																													
Name 2																													
Name 3																													

TUESDAY

TIME	7:00	7:30	8:00	8:30	9:00	9:30	10:00	10:30	11:00	11:30	12:00	12:30	1:00	1:30	2:00	2:30	3:00	3:30	4:00	4:30	5:00	5:30	6:00	6:30	7:00	7:30	8:00	8:30	9:00
						AM															PM								
Name 1																													
Name 2																													
Name 3																													

WEDNESDAY

TIME	7:00	7:30	8:00	8:30	9:00	9:30	10:00	10:30	11:00	11:30	12:00	12:30	1:00	1:30	2:00	2:30	3:00	3:30	4:00	4:30	5:00	5:30	6:00	6:30	7:00	7:30	8:00	8:30	9:00
						AM															PM								
Name 1																													
Name 2																													
Name 3																													

THURSDAY

TIME	7:00	7:30	8:00	8:30	9:00	9:30	10:00	10:30	11:00	11:30	12:00	12:30	1:00	1:30	2:00	2:30	3:00	3:30	4:00	4:30	5:00	5:30	6:00	6:30	7:00	7:30	8:00	8:30	9:00
						AM															PM								
Name 1																													
Name 2																													
Name 3																													

FRIDAY

TIME	7:00	7:30	8:00	8:30	9:00	9:30	10:00	10:30	11:00	11:30	12:00	12:30	1:00	1:30	2:00	2:30	3:00	3:30	4:00	4:30	5:00	5:30	6:00	6:30	7:00	7:30	8:00	8:30	9:00
						AM															PM								
Name 1																													
Name 2																													
Name 3																													

SATURDAY

TIME	7:00	7:30	8:00	8:30	9:00	9:30	10:00	10:30	11:00	11:30	12:00	12:30	1:00	1:30	2:00	2:30	3:00	3:30	4:00	4:30	5:00	5:30	6:00	6:30	7:00	7:30	8:00	8:30	9:00
						AM															PM								
Name 1																													
Name 2																													
Name 3																													

SUNDAY

TIME	7:00	7:30	8:00	8:30	9:00	9:30	10:00	10:30	11:00	11:30	12:00	12:30	1:00	1:30	2:00	2:30	3:00	3:30	4:00	4:30	5:00	5:30	6:00	6:30	7:00	7:30	8:00	8:30	9:00
						AM															PM								
Name 1																													
Name 2																													
Name 3																													
TOTALS																													

KEY
1. Relaxed times
2. Stressed times
3. Most energetic times
4. Times when most tasks are accomplished and when productivity is at an all-time high.

I realize that this seems like a lot of work, but you will inevitably encounter trends that you never realized until you do this charting. I discovered that my daughter was more productive doing her homework in the morning before school rather than after school. I also found out that adding a breakfast snack to Kenneth's backpack helped ease the stress of his mornings.

Equipped with this information and some fine-tuning, your family's days should have fewer glitches. A schedule is a major component for your success in time management. We all know that we can never get time back, and using it wisely is God's will for our lives. Doing this step first will add to the proficiency of your schedule.

Walk in wisdom toward outsiders, making the best use of the time.

Colossians 4:5 (ESV)

So teach us to number our days,
that we may get a heart of wisdom.

Psalms 90:12 (ESV)

Making the best use of the time, because the days are evil.

Ephesians 5:16 (ESV)

Pray for God's guidance. Then, using the productivity chart, create a schedule that incorporates your vision for your family rather than scribbling down random goals.

If it is worship time with God, the reflection of its significance needs to be evident in your actions. Our children must see us worship, read our Bible, and seek Jesus if it is a priority. It is up to us to demonstrate the vision for the family.

Decide what is important. God will give you the desires of your heart. It may help to review your parent plan. A good plan will have your vision, desires, and goals written out. Refer to them prior to creating your schedule. Jot down a list using your goals and desires.

- My child's life would reflect the love of Jesus
- My child would discover his talents
- My child would walk in her purpose
- My child...

Your list may not look like it may be made into a schedule at this time, but we are working up to that. These desires and your goals may seem monumental on the surface. However, once composed into your family schedule they will seem attainable.

Here is a method along with my schedule that helped me to be more purposeful in raising my children. I refer to it as the

KEYS to success. KEYS is an acronym that may help transition you to a different mindset—and victory will be closer than you might have perceived.

<u>K</u>indness is the best way to develop a relationship, and relationships are essential in intentional parenting.

My mom often restated the old adage, *"You catch more flies with honey than you do with vinegar."*

But the fruit of the Spirit is love, joy, peace, forbearance, kindness, goodness, faithfulness, gentleness, and self-control.
Against such things there is no law.
Galatians 5:22-23 (NIV)

A gentle answer turns away wrath, but a harsh word stirs up anger.
Proverbs 15:1 (NIV)

<u>E</u>rase Mistakes. This is why someone invented an eraser. An eraser erases mistakes and allows the correction to cover the mistake without any evidence of the wrong.

<u>Y</u>es. Find ways to say "yes." *Yes* encourages your child's strongest efforts and helps him to reach his potential.

<u>S</u>tand Firm. Stand your ground, stay consistent.

I wanted my child's life to reflect the love of Jesus. I used the KEYS, and I am overjoyed to attest that my children have a heart for God; it shows in the way that they treat others.

Kindness

The definition of kindness is: *the quality of being friendly, generous, and considerate.*

If you desire your child's life to reflect the love of Jesus, you must work enthusiastically to have your life reflect the love of Jesus. You must hang out with our Lord and Savior. Our relationship with Him allows us to love and show kindness.

I am by no means implying that I have been a reflection of God's amazing love at all times, although I can claim that I did have some good moments that were glimpses of me reflecting His love. Those times were glorious, and the reward from them left me striving for more.

This is where the hard work comes in. I'm not saying that hanging out with God is hard. Rather, it's the making the time to do it that is difficult.

I use the words *hanging out with God* because I want to express that this is informal time that you spend with God—your friend and the great *I Am*. It doesn't include petitioning Him for your wants. It is the time that you allow Him to do most of the talking.

As a parent I try do what is important, but sometimes I have chosen to do things that net me immediate results rather than things that I know are best for me, but that take a long time to see the fruits of my labors. This is why we must schedule our time and stick to that schedule. Good things take time to develop.

The more time I spent with God, the easier it was to be kind. And kindness is not one of my strongest attributes. Time with Him cultivates kindness, compassion, and generosity.

Set an appointment with God that works well for you. Note this time on your family schedule. It doesn't have to be first thing in the morning. Be consistent, but if you miss your appointment, give yourself some grace. This is not just about you, it's also about your children and what God is doing through you.

Help your child set a daily appointment with God, not only prayers at bedtime. A chart with stickers, a journal, or an app on your phone all work as excellent tools to build consistency. Consider using a sticker on the chart each time your young child follows through with his scheduled time with God.

Activities, when scheduled and consistently, done are much more likely to transform into an unconscious habit. Good habits are better than after-the-fact lectures.

Look for opportunities for your child to practice random acts of kindness. Make this intentional by including this on your family schedule as well. If it is on a schedule, the family is ten times more likely to do it. When your children are young this may be more your responsibility than theirs.

Start with an outreach that touches your heart in your service to others. Encourage your children to join you in your efforts to bring kindness to others. Once a month volunteer to feed the homeless or shovel a senior's driveway. As your child becomes old enough, allow her to choose what she wishes to do. The goal is for your child to take over the duty of facilitating acts of kindness.

The important thing is to write it down. It is part of the plan. Use a calendar, and schedule monthly acts of kindness for the entire year or add it to your family schedule. If something happens that doesn't allow your child to do what was scheduled, he may perform another act of kindness on a different day during that same month.

Don't pick arbitrary acts, rather talk with your child about how her actions will impact the recipient. Discuss why serving others is beneficial.

You may begin this activity with children as young as three years of age, depending on your child's understanding. Start simple. Allow your child to take toys that he no longer plays with to a children's center. A five-year-old could make a few sandwiches for the homeless. Choose acts of kindness that resonate with your child's heart. Once your child is mature enough to take on this responsibility, consistently let him.

Each child will mature in this area at a different age. Look for signs that exhibit the ability to organize and carry out strategic plans. Most children entering middle school will be eager to accept the challenge. This is an excellent time to rejoice in the extra time that you will gain as your child is used for God's glory!

Stop scheduling the acts of kindness once your child is performing them with consistency on her own. Now write down all of the opportunities that God gives her to bless someone else. If your child performs random acts of kindness less than once a month, return to scheduling them.

I will never forget one special day when Kenneth and I were coming home from church. We drove down a somewhat busy street on a sunny spring day after 18 inches of heavy, wet snow had fallen the night before. We saw a small-framed, short, whited-haired woman bent over shoveling her sidewalk. Kenneth spotted her first.

He was 12 years old and insisted that I stop the car. I didn't have a place to pull over and didn't want to impede traffic. Hearing Kenneth's pleas, I stopped and let him out of the car. I turned the emergency flasher on. Nicole, Kenneth's two-year-old sister, and I waited in the car.

The deep snow didn't discourage Kenneth. He stepped in the holes in the snow where other people had left footprints. Kenneth jumped from footprint to footprint all the way to the old lady to avoid getting snow in his brown church shoes. I saw him tug at her snow shovel. She shook her head.

Kenneth stopped pulling on her shovel and was now talking while his hand rested on her shovel. He had a gorgeous smile, and he used it to its full brilliance. I saw the woman hug him, as he once again tried to take her shovel.

This went on for five minutes. Kenneth then bounced back to the car with a confused look on his face.

"What happened?" I quizzed Kenneth with an eagerness that covered the suspense permeating the car.

"She wants to shovel her own snow. She refused my help. She told me that shoveling was her exercise on a sunny Sunday morning."

I smiled inside and out and expressed how proud I was of him for trying to help her. It was the first of many times without any prompting from me that he chose to be kind to a stranger. Kenneth performed many more awesome acts of kindness as he began to walk in his purpose.

Kindness isn't just about works. It is about how we interact with others. And one way we interact is through how we lead others. There are many ways to influence your child to do what they know they should do. Kindness helps us explain why it is important for someone to do something in a way that allows him to readily receive the order. If we want something done, there should be a reason. Kindness takes a moment to help others understand why. This is particularly important in parenting.

When I was a child, this concept was rejected by the seniors in my life; if you questioned why you had to do something, it was deemed disrespectful and rude. Parents in my day made comments like, "*Do it now, because I said so.*"

Taking that moment to help a child comprehend *why* is an expression of kindness. Kindness is love. It empathizes with how others feel and builds them up. Our interactions with others should express compassion for them in all areas of their lives.

Put on then, as God's chosen ones, holy and beloved, compassionate hearts, kindness, humility, meekness, and patience.

Colossians 3:12 (NIV)

She opens her mouth with wisdom, and the teaching of kindness is on her tongue.

Proverbs 31:26 (ESV)

Love is patient and kind; love does not envy or boast; it is not arrogant or rude.

1 Corinthians 13:4 (ESV)

Erase Mistakes

Erasing mistakes is grace, but for me it's easier to understand the word grace. Grace in biblical terms can refer to a level of forgiveness, repentance, regeneration, and salvation. A common definition describes grace as the unmerited favor of God toward man. It is being given favor when you deserve to be found guilty and punished. We all need grace but often forget to extend it. Our children will mess up, and so will we.

Brothers and sisters, I know that I still have a long way to go. But there is one thing I do: I forget what is in the past and try as hard as I can to reach the goal before me.

Philippians 3:13 (NIV)

Mistake (n):

    an action or judgment that is misguided or wrong.

Mistakes are just that—wrong—so move on, erase the mistake, and correct it by moving forward with the intention of never doing it again. Remember to *embrace the erase*. This is grace.

I would like to give you my simple example of the meaning of grace using spilled milk. If I spill the milk while trying to pour myself a glass, after my mom warned me that the milk carton was too heavy for me, I have made a mistake. I used bad judgment and made a mess. I need to clean up the milk and ask for some help to pour a new glass of milk.

Yes, it is wise for my mom to point out the connection between my poor choice and the expense of spilling the milk. She may also tell me ways to avoid this in the future. She could tell me about the cost in terms of time spent cleaning up the mess and about how time is precious. Money was wasted on the milk that is all over the floor and table. She may instruct me to hold the milk carton for a few extra seconds next time to see if the weight is too heavy for me.

However, after she points out the cost and ways to avoid the mistake in the future, she must allow my failed attempt to be erased and the correction of the mistake to be enough. The evidence of the mistake is erased when I cleaned up the milk and she poured me a new glass of milk. They must receive it as a lesson learned and moved on. That's right, don't cry over spilled milk.

This is so important because we want our children to try new things and sometimes reach beyond their comfort level. If too much emphasis is put on the mistakes that they make, they will fear even calculated risk. Life has risk, and taking chances is part of life.

Use the eraser often.

My daughter Nicole was born spirited, and sometimes she questioned me with such intensity that it bordered on rudeness. On good days I could redirect her kindly to rephrase her questions to be respectful. Other days I failed. In those days we reviewed where she messed up and where I messed up and erased the event going forward with a correction of how it should have been done. We learned and couldn't look back at what was gone (erased). Showing grace and mercy is a reflection of **God's** love.

Be merciful, even as your Father is merciful.

Luke 6:36 (ESV)

Blessed are the merciful, for they shall receive mercy.

Matthew 5:7 (ESV)

> *But by the free gift of God's grace all are put right with Him through Christ Jesus, who sets them free.*
>
> Romans 3:24 (GNT)

Yes

Say it often! The word *No* shouldn't be allowed to penetrate our children's souls. I hear *No* too often from many parents. It is important to find ways to say *Yes*. This is a challenge at times, but it is worth the long-term results.

When our children were young, my husband and I learned to keep our vocabulary simple. We wanted them to understand. We wanted to keep them safe, so we echoed *No* a lot. When we didn't want them to hit others, we barked *No*. We knew that they understood the word *No*, and as a result they responded quickly and appropriately. We loved the word because of its effectiveness, so we used it often. It was the easiest and fastest way to halt unwanted behavior.

The over-use of the word *No* tells our children more than some of us may realize. Children are born to be inquisitive, that is how God made them. So, when they're putting that dirty rock in their mouth, they are trying to learn. *What is this? What does it taste like? Is it edible?*

When we scream *No*, we are essentially declaring, *No learning. No exploring. You are not allowed to discover new things.* This is not the message that we want to send to our children. Consider using the word *No* much less frequently. Try re-directing young children to a choice that they can explore. A growing child needs you to replace that *No* with *Yes*.

If your child is doing something that you don't approve of, take time to explain the reason for your disapproval. Will what she is doing hurt her or someone else? This will help her process the cause and effect of her behavior. Always look for moments to teach your child to think and reason out her actions.

In the old days this was called common sense. Remember, the more opportunities we give children to think, the better their skills develop at doing it. Reply with a *Yes*, and let your children help you work out the details to an option that would otherwise have elicited a *No*. This is an excellent way to build a child's reasoning skills.

An easy way to practice this approach is to ask your child a few questions rather than immediately blurting out *No* to something that might hurt him. *"Why do you want to do that? Can you get hurt doing that? Is there any other way that you can still accomplish what you want that has less of a risk of getting hurt?"*

When a child maneuvers through this process and discovers a safer way of achieving what he wants, respond with *Yes*. "Yes, I think that that is a winning idea that you have."

No Perfect Parent, Just a Perfect Purpose

Hearing *Yes* often builds confidence and reassurance in our children. In our world now, many people suffer from insecurity and low self-esteem. People with these conditions find it difficult to reflect love and kindness. They often hurt others. Build up your child with the word *Yes* as often as possible. *Yes* encourages success.

> *Behind every young child who believes in himself is a parent who believed first.*
> — Matthew Jacobson, Historian

> *My doctors told me that I would never walk again. My mother told me that I would. I believed my mother.*
> — Wilma Rudolph, Olympian

Even as children grow older, still find ways to avoid planting the word *No* into their spirit. I have a cute *Yes* story to share.

Nicole, at 14 years old, had long, black hair and a shy but sassy personality. She wore a size two. Being five feet, six inches tall, with curves in all the right places, she drew admiring eyes from many. Her innocent, baby-looking face and smile lit up any room. All of her adorable attributes made it hard to say *No*. And my responsibility as a good mom obliged me to find ways to utter *Yes* as much as possible.

Nicole called me one Thursday evening on my way home from work. "Mom, can I go over to my friend Brian's house and watch movies tomorrow after school? We have a half-day at school and Brain invited a few friends over."

Brian was a classmate that Nicole had mentioned a few times, but I hadn't met him. I had had a long day, and this caught me off guard. This was Nicole's first year at this school, and she didn't have many friends that I was aware of.

I questioned if she had discussed this idea with her dad and what his answer was.

Nicole imitated her dad's voice in a deep, gruff tone. "'Absolutely not!' But he told me to ask you."

Good, his response was no. This took some of the burden off of me.

"Let's discuss it when I get home."

The rest of my drive was filled with thoughts of how I could respond with a *Yes* to her. Nicole didn't ask for many things. She had never requested to hang out with friends before. When I arrived home I had a conversation with her dad. He advised me to use my motherly judgement and make the call.

I then interrogated Nicole. "Will Brian's parents be at home?"

"No, but his older sister will be there."

"How much older?"

"She's a senior."

She meant that the girl was only in the 12th grade, a few years older than she was.

Little girl, are you nuts? I kept that thought where it belonged, in my head.

I then pressed her for more information. "Who else will be there? Could I meet Brian's parents?"

She tried to further her argument. "Brian's parents work a lot, but Brian's cousin Alex will also be there."

"How old is Brian's cousin?"

Nicole avoided eye contact with me and retorted, "He is the same age as me."

At that instant, God's wisdom showed itself, and I heard, "*Tell her 'Yes.'*"

So I proclaimed, "Yes, Nicole you can go."

This might seem unwise or odd to some readers that I would allow my daughter to go hang out with two boys and a somewhat older sister. It was odd for me too.

Nicole sensed my apprehension. "Mom, don't you trust me?"

"Nicole, it's not you who I don't trust. I don't have confidence in people I don't know to make sure that you are safe."

Nicole shot back. "I know what to do if things get out of hand."

Looking at her, I knew that she believed that, but I wasn't sure that she knew all of the important aspects of what could happen in this case to make a wise choice.

Well, the facts were that I trusted her, but I didn't know the other kids well enough to trust them. I submitted the *Yes* because I wanted her to have fun watching movies with her friends. My job was to keep her safe while still being able to offer her a *Yes*.

"Yes, I trust you, and you can go."

I didn't trust the boys, so I handled that as a separate issue. I told Nicole that I would pick her up from school and take her to Brian's house. I wanted to know where he lived.

After school the next day, as promised, I picked her and her friends up. I drove them to Brian's house. This way I was able to meet them before the movies. The friends were much different than I expected. These were the boys that my daughter would be alone watching movies with for hours.

I was thinking that these boys would be small, skinny, smart, and nerdy-looking. They were in the International Baccalaureate (IB) program at school. The IB program presented a rigorous academic challenge with college level classes. The truth of the matter was that I visualized smart kids as all looking the same. I was wrong.

These boys may have been smart, but they were not little, nerdy-looking, or skinny. They were the picture of healthy, young men, with the emphasis on *men*. They had facial hair and defined muscle tone.

My stomach fluttered, but I was committed to my *Yes*. I drove Nicole, Alex, and Brian to Brian's house. I parked the car, and the guys jumped out and bolted to the front door of Brian's home. Nicole sat in the front passenger seat. Before she opened the car door, I implored her to call me if she needed me. I would be right outside. Nicole smiled and bounced out of the car. She seemed to skip down the sidewalk to the door with light, rhythmic steps.

I did just what I obligated myself to do. I waited outside the entire time. I did some reading, and I prayed that God would keep Nicole safe.

When Nicole was in the house the boys questioned whether her mom really intended to wait outside the whole time. She confidently exclaimed *Yes*. Later, Nicole divulged that detail to me.

Brian and Alex kept peeping through the white mini blinds on the window in the front door. They checked to see if I was still waiting in my car. I waved and grinned at them, and they quickly disappeared. The blinds continued to move for a few moments after they were gone. I apparently took on the role of being part of the entertainment for the day.

They checked every 20 minutes or so and then reported to Nicole that I was still there. After an hour and a half my daughter pranced out of the house.

Nicole giggled and beamed. "The guys thought that you were funny, Mom. You are pretty silly, but I know you care about me."

I conceded the point. "I will take that as a compliment."

"Mom! Brain's mom made us the best egg rolls I ever tasted. All the snacks were so good." Nicole raved about the event.

I interrupted her. "Was his mother home?"

"No," Nicole's face lit up as she recounted her hour-and-a-half of fun. "I almost missed some of the movie because the guys kept jumping up and sliding in their socks over to the window to look at you. Alex slipped and fell. Mom! Brian admitted that he didn't think you would stay out there the whole time. I told them that you would."

Her excitement was well worth the *Yes* that I had given her.

I later got to know Alex and Brian quite well, but her friends discovered something that day. Those boys learned that Nicole had a protective mom, that I loved her dearly, and that I was willing to do whatever was necessary to keep her safe.

Brian and Alex shared with me that they were slightly afraid of me. I believe that seeing my will to shield my daughter at any cost established a respect for our family aspirations. I was glad that they had this epiphany.

Nicole never asked to do that again, however, which was okay by me. This is not to say that she didn't want to hang out with her friends anymore. Nicole just found ways to do this that were more comfortable for her parents to accept. She made sure that parents would be at home during gatherings and that her dad and I knew her friends.

Don't forget, when you say *Yes*, you encourage success! Appeal to God to help you find ways to say *Yes* more often.

This situation might seem extreme to some, but in whatever situation in which you find yourself, be creative, listen, pray, and do what God tells you to do. Our God is a *Yes* God, and when we find ways to allow a *Yes*, it is a reflection of His love.

Stand Firm

Standing firm is just another way of motivating you to be consistent. This also may be hard work, but if you invest the time, the results of your efforts will be worthwhile.

Our children find ways to push the boundaries. I think it's their job. Our job is to stand firm even when we get discouraged. If you have decided what is best for your child, don't change your mind when he puts you to the test. Yes, every child is different, and so are the ways in which he will challenge the boundaries.

I think that it is important to set boundaries that stand up to tough reasoning as to why the rule is in place. You likely have heard it said that we need to pick our battles. This is a wise adage. Don't fight a battle simply to make your life easier or because of pride.

My friend, Keshia, once dug her feet in about her son taking out the trash on Thursday night. She didn't want to be flexible in this situation. She confided to me that it was easier for her to pull out of the garage if the trash can was on the curb on Friday mornings because she had to be to work early and often ran late.

Her nine-year-old son, Josh, wanted to take the trash out on Friday morning on his way to school.

Josh complained about this every week. "It doesn't make sense to take the trash out at night. I always have to take out the additional trash that everyone makes in the morning, anyway."

As an onlooker, I could see that it was not optimal for Josh to take the trash out on Thursday.

He also mentioned that it was hard to see at night and that he was scared.

Keshia's rationale could not stand up to what was best for Josh. Letting Josh take the trash out in the morning meant that he could see better, do it only once, and not be scared. It also allowed the rest of the family an opportunity to gather up last minute trash in the morning. Although this didn't make life easier for Keshia, it maybe should have been a battle that she was willing to let go of. Stand firm on battles for which you believe you know the best outcome, and be flexible when it makes sense.

Parenting is hard work, but the value of a child raised for their glorious purpose is priceless. You are cultivating greatness. And with that comes immense responsibility. You want your child not to agree with things because you say so but rather because she sees the value in your wisdom. A child who agrees because it is what is best will continue to look for the best plan even when you aren't around. Encourage this thought process because there will be many times when you aren't there to guide him through what's best.

Stand firm. Bolster yourself to not be moved. Remind yourself that consistency gives children a strong foundation on which to stand. There is no balance to an always-moving mandate. When you implement a rule, don't knock your child off balance by changing it or allowing it to lapse. Consistency offers your child security and a strong anchor as she casts her nets into deep water. Consistency also helps you when the storms of parenting threaten to engulf you. Stand firm. Be strong.

Be on your guard; stand firm in the faith; be courageous; be strong.

1 Corinthians 16:13 (NIV)

*You will not have to fight this battle. Take up your positions; stand firm and see the deliverance the L*ORD *will give you, Judah and Jerusalem. Do not be afraid; do not be discouraged. Go out to face them tomorrow, and the L*ORD *will be with you.*

2 Chronicles 20:17 (NIV)

You are now ready to create a schedule that includes what is important to the success of the family vision. Start from the time that your child wakes up and end when he goes to bed. I suggest using a calendar posted in a central location. If members of the family are older, maybe using Google calendar is a nice option. It is easy to update and set reminders. Use the KEYS to help implement your family's desires and values. Lastly, remember to be the example of what you want others in your family to be.

RECAP

- Write down your parenting plan.
- Create a family schedule that works *best* for your family.
- Use the KEYS:

    Kindness

    Erase Mistakes

    Yes

    Stand Firm.

CHAPTER FOUR

Get Help!

You are never strong enough that you don't need help.

— Cesar Chavez

Be willing to admit that you don't know the answer but that it is likely that someone else does. Find that person! As you navigate through your parenting journey, life will present problems to which you don't have the answers. There are people out there who are willing to share what they have learned. I believe that God has placed people in our path ready to help us just when we need them the most. Be willing to ask for help, and then accept it.

When Kenneth was two years old, we moved next door to a second-grade school teacher. She taught me what books were suitable to read to a toddler. She suggested that I make sounds and use facial expressions to keep Kenneth interested when I read to him. She poured a wealth of information into me. She showed me helpful ways to teach and engage Kenneth that were age-appropriate.

I bought lots of books and read to my baby every day. My neighbor divulged that she often saw children of color enter kindergarten with skills far behind those of the other students. She mentioned that she had read an article stating that children of color start with fewer than 1,800 words when entering kindergarten when they should have between 2,100 and 2,200 vocabulary words. She revealed that they struggled with sentence structure and with fine motor skills—essential for learning to write properly with a pencil.

I recall thinking that I couldn't let those things become an issue for my child. I visited the library, purchased, and read many parenting books about preparing children to be successful in school.

Many times, I didn't have the answers as to what to do when my children were sick, refused to go to bed, or didn't want to eat. I usually called my mom first. Her wisdom and knowledge had come from many previous generations and from her own experience raising three children. And when she didn't have the answer, she directed me to call the doctor.

Determining when it is time to seek help should come easily, but sometimes pride may be blinding. My mother taught me that if I didn't have the answer, I should find someone who did. This concept has been a huge part of my life in many areas.

When I was a student in school, I went home one day not understanding my homework.

Mom's voice came at me stern and direct. "Why didn't you request instructions you could understand from your teacher?"

Mom wanted to make sure that I was clear about her expectations for me to do well in school, and that meant that I needed to be able to do the work.

She scolded me, "If you couldn't figure out the answers, there were others in the class who couldn't solve the problems, either. If you had asked questions, you would not only have helped yourself, you would have helped your classmates too."

I took this lesson to heart.

As you have probably noticed, I like to assist my memory by using acronyms. So, naturally, we must include the following acronym to remind you to ASK.

Always

Seek

Knowledge

> *The heart of the discerning acquires knowledge,*
> *for the ears of the wise seek it out.*
>
> Proverbs 18:15 (NIV)

Teaching my children to search for the answers was one of the most impactful lessons that I passed on to them. Kenneth is a published mathematician and an orthopedic surgeon. He has a master's degree in medical bioengineering and worked as a high school math teacher and quantitative analyst before becoming an orthopedic surgeon as a resident at Yale New Haven Hospital. I share this to let you know that by the time Kenneth was in fourth grade, his math skills had surpassed his mom's knowledge, and I couldn't help him do his math homework anymore.

Of course, I passed on to him the wise words of my mom. I told him that he had better not come home without the ability to understand and complete all of his homework. Yes, I roared that with some attitude because it was that important. I wanted to make sure that he grasped the magnitude of what was vital to his personal victories in life.

We had a drawn-out discussion about the requirements of his teacher's job. She received a monthly salary to teach him. If he left that school without the necessary information to complete his assignments, his teacher had failed. I drilled into him the lesson that the teacher must teach him and that he must try to understand, so that neither of them failed.

A quiet, sweet, and shy child, Kenneth didn't like attention. I used role play to build his confidence. I practiced with him ways that he might approach his teacher when he needed more

Get Help!

information to understand a concept being taught. I emphasized that it was imperative that his method be respectful and polite. I admonished and encouraged him daily to use his wonderful charm. I told him to smile and be engaging.

I instructed that he look the teacher in the eyes and speak in a clear manner loud enough for her to hear him. I directed him to make sure to include information in his questions that the teacher had discussed in the lesson to show that he had been paying attention.

Yes, all of this fastidious detail and preparation with a nine-year-old year old little brown boy was necessary. Why? Because I was aware that the odds were against him. I wanted Kenneth to have a chance at being whatever he wanted to be when he grew up. I embraced the fact that I was on a mission of raising greatness. Kenneth needed to have the skills to petition his teacher to gain the answers to questions that he didn't know. He needed to be persistent and resilient.

These life lessons continued with my daughter. When Nicole was in kindergarten, she brought a homework assignment home and needed help. I did help her, and she missed every single answer. The sad thing about this is that I was indeed trying to get the answers right. This reminded me that I was out of my lane. My job was not to do her homework but to teach her how to do it on her own. I decided that it was time to teach Nicole the homework lesson sooner than I had taught it to Kenneth because of a major mom fail.

Nicole could write her full name by age three and spell and recognize many complex words. Nicole was reading at third grade level by the age of four and had excellent basic addition and subtraction skills. She was meticulous about every assignment and project. Her favorite home game was me assigning her pretend school homework like her brother. She loved learning and achieving. I disclose all of this so that you may understand that missing every answer on her homework paper in kindergarten was devastating to this little perfectionist.

So, we had *the discussion* at age five about what the teacher's responsibility was and what hers was.

"Look, it wasn't *my* responsibility to get the answers right, it was *yours*! You left the classroom without understanding the assignment. Your teacher is there to teach you. Her job is to make sure that you understand what is required and how to do it. If you don't understand the assignment before you leave the class, you allow both you and your teacher to fail," I lectured her.

I still see in my mind to this day her brown eyes filling with tears. "Because of you, I missed all of the answers!"

We spent an entire week reconditioning her thinking. I told her that she had missed the answers because of herself. On the way to the park, in between songs and laughter, I coached Nicole on what she had to do when she was at school. She repeated that she needed to understand her assignments before she left the classroom. I then cheered and high-fived my daughter.

In both our fun moments and our serious moments I rehearsed with her the mandatory steps for classroom success as a chant, and she echoed it back to me. It was a lesson she learned well, and she never came home with homework for me to help her with ever again. But perhaps you already figured that one out.

Seeking wisdom doesn't stop with school or medical attention. It should encompass all areas of life. There are many excellent parenting books specific to most every area of parenting that one might tussle with. You might consider buying what you need.

And never underestimate the wisdom of an experienced mom. It never hurts to seek her counsel. If you don't like her advice, keep quiet, and don't use it. That way you will keep the lines of communication open, and you can use what you want and dismiss what may not be helpful to you.

I once heard a new mom, with irritation in her voice, protest that she didn't want the advice of her mother-in-law. Annoyed, she complained that her mother-in-law had gotten to make her own mistakes and now she wanted the chance to make her own mistakes too. These statements perplexed me. *What a prideful and silly thing to believe. She can learn from her mother-in-law and still make her own mistakes.*

Parenting is way too difficult for you not to misjudge, overreact, or screw up many times during the journey. It is wise to listen to advice offered. Trust me, you will have plenty of opportunities to mess up on your own. Don't let pride keep you from being the blessing that your child needs.

The way of fools seems right to them, but the wise listen to advice.
Proverbs 12:15 (NIV)

Where there is strife, there is pride, but wisdom is found in those who take advice.
Proverbs 13:10 (NIV)

Listen to advice and accept discipline, and at the end you will be counted among the wise.
Proverbs 19:20 (NIV)

Be on the hunt for opportunities to seek wisdom. If your child is having problems in school, don't be ashamed to reach out to other parents in the class whose children are doing well. Dedicate some time to gathering information about what might be some factors to their child's success. Consider asking questions like, "How long does your child study?" and "What do they believe is the key to their child's success?" The answer could be as simple as increasing study time for your own child.

Talk to the teacher. Spend time observing in the classroom. Can you understand what the teacher is requesting from the students? I recognize that this may be difficult for working parents, but it is a prerequisite to raising greatness.

Visiting your child's school unannounced two to three times during a semester presents the teacher with evidence of your desire to see your child do well. It often gives her more of an incentive to help you achieve this goal. This may only be necessary once during the school year if your child is doing well in school. I suggest just once in the first year for middle school students. High school students may not need this kind of support.

I love the well-known African proverb that states, *"It takes a village to raise a child."* Find friends, and recruit family members to be a part of your village. Appeal for help from everyone you know and accept the help from all of those willing to give it. Eat well, get plenty of rest, and try to stay healthy. Perhaps you could use those sick days for school visits.

Help your child set up an organizational system in which he blocks off when and where he will do his homework. Take time to add fun, inspirational personal touches to his work space. In collaboration with your child, create an accountability-structured system, and add it to the schedule.

One way to accomplish this is by adding signature areas to the calendar. Then have your child get a signature from a designated person to verify that the work has been performed.

Adding playful alarm sounds, fun calendars, and color-coded checklists may create some needed enthusiasm. Don't forget to look for clues for when it is time for kids to be responsible for their own schedules, and appropriately allow them to take over small bits at a time. The goal is for them to oversee their daily schedules completely.

Lastly, I believe in a reward system, which some may conclude is bribery. I call it life's bonuses. When I work, I am financially compensated. Yes, the quality of my work is to glorify God, but I do happily accept monetary remuneration, bonuses, and gifts when presented with them.

I referred to school work as my children's job. The compensation that they received at school was the knowledge that they gained and a sense of accomplishment. The reward and bonuses were the extra goodies and praise that they received from their dad and mom. Most of us appreciate when others recognize our hard work and being rewarded for a job well done.

RECAP

- ASK others for help.
- Visit schools regularly.
- Set up a schedule and a place and a time for homework.
- Acknowledge your child's success.

CHAPTER FIVE

NITRO = Explosive Love

Loving big requires an explosive love. It is the kind of love that blows away unforgiveness. It shatters malice and envy. It destroys record-keeping of wrongdoings, quick tempers, boasting, and bitterness. Loving big is a heart condition. It is impossible without God's dynamic power. Consider utilizing nitroglycerin to be an effective lover of all.

Nitroglycerin, also called glyceryl trinitrate, is a powerful explosive and an important ingredient in most forms of dynamite. It is also used with nitrocellulose in some propellants, especially for rockets and missiles, and it is employed as a vasodilator in the easing of cardiac pain.

In short, nitro may be used to blow up a bridge, thrust a rocket into space, or to ease the pain of hurting hearts. Allow NITRO to blow up the bridges of divisions in your relationships and heal the heart hurts that will inevitably come your way. I have an acronym for NITRO too!

Never give up on love.

Interrupt negative thoughts with positive ones.

Trust God and meditate on His word.

Reconciliation is always the goal.

Overlook offenses and go above and beyond what you feel.

Love never gives up, never loses faith, is always hopeful, and endures through every circumstance.

1 Corinthians 13:7 (NLT)

Never Give Up On Love

- **No** pain, no gain.
- **Nothing** worth having is easy.

God warned us that we do not know Him if we do not love. We must love and never give up because love never fails.

Beloved, let us love one another, for love is from God, and whoever loves has been born of God and knows God.

1 John 4:7 (ESV)

Whoever does not love does not know God, because God is love.

1 John 4:8 (ESV)

Love is much more than an emotion—it is a combination of taking control of our feelings and ordering our will to comply with what is best for someone other than ourselves. It obliges us to commit to working hard, to being selfless, and to many other challenges—some easy and some difficult. In the difficult times, we focus on God's love for us. God commands us to love.

Love must be sincere. Hate what is evil; cling to what is good.
Be devoted to one another in love.
Honor one another above yourselves.

Romans 12:9-10 (NIV)

Love is patient and kind; love does not envy or boast;
it is not arrogant or rude. It does not insist on its own way;
it is not irritable or resentful; it does not rejoice at wrongdoing,
but rejoices with the truth.
Love bears all things, believes all things,
hopes all things, endures all things.

1 Corinthians 13:4-7 ESV)

Interrupt Negative Thoughts With Positive Ones

How do we do this?

- **Intensify** your praise.
- **Identity** check: You are a child of God.
- **Imagine** God-driven outcomes.

Finally, brothers and sisters, whatever is true, whatever is noble, whatever is right, whatever is pure, whatever is lovely, whatever is admirable— if anything is excellent or praiseworthy—think about such things.

Philippians 4:8 (The Living Bible)

Those who live according to the flesh have their minds set on what the flesh desires; but those who live in accordance with the Spirit have their minds set on what the Spirit desires.

Romans 8:5 (NIV)

We demolish arguments and every pretension that sets itself up against the knowledge of God, and we take captive every thought to make it obedient to Christ.

2 Corinthians 10:5 (NIV)

Trust God, and Meditate On His Word

- **Take** it to God, and believe that He will take care of it and you.

Give your burdens to the LORD, and He will take care of you.
He will not permit the godly to slip and fall.

Psalms 55:22 (NLT)

Trust in the LORD with all your heart and lean not on your own understanding; in all your ways submit to Him, and He will make your paths straight.

Proverbs 3:5-6 (NIV)

Whoever gives heed to instruction prospers, and blessed is the one who trusts in the LORD.

Proverbs 16:20 (NIV)

LORD Almighty, blessed is the one who trusts in you.

Psalms 84:12 (NIV)

*Many are the woes of the wicked, but the L*ORD*'s unfailing love surrounds the one who trusts in Him.*

Psalms 32:10 (NIV)

*Trust in the L*ORD *and do good.
Then you will live safely in the land and prosper.*

Psalms 37:3 (NLT)

*Those who trust in the L*ORD *are like Mount Zion, which cannot be shaken but endures forever.*

Psalms 125:1 (NIV)

Thank God.

*Be thankful in all circumstances,
for this is God's will for you who belong to Christ Jesus.*

1 Thessalonians 5:18 (NLT)

God wants us to trust that He has our best interests in mind in every situation. When you feel hopeless and immobilized by pain, listen quietly to His voice. The situation may not change immediately, but how you feel should. If you can't hear His sweet words of encouragement, praise Him and listen again. Praise with a sincere heart, lift Him up with a song and words that may be heard by your ears.

Take one step at a time. Don't look beyond the next moment. Allow God to direct you minute by minute. Don't think about what will happen next or what needs to be done later, just praise. When you make it through, stop and realize the power and the care that your Father has for you. Think about how sweetly He encourages us when we need it most.

Reconciliation Is Always The Goal

- **Responsibility** is mine!
- **Remind** myself of my purpose. (Knowing that I am a child of the King of Kings and Lord of Lords helps me to focus on what I was created to do.)

We were all born self-focused and sinners, therefore, showing love constantly is impossible. We are flawed human beings. We will cause others pain, sometimes intentionally, sometimes without thought, and sometimes out of our own attempt to persevere through life challenges. With all of the hurts that we all are confronted with, and will continue to experience as we live, we must master forgiveness and the art of reconciliation. Loving big requires us to take on the responsibility of being ministers of reconciliation.

Reconciling a relationship comes with its own set of challenges. Allow God to lead you through the process, and if necessary, seek professional help.

So from now on we regard no one from a worldly point of view. Though we once regarded Christ in this way, we do so no longer. Therefore, if anyone is in Christ, the new creation has come: The old has gone, the new is here! All this is from God, who reconciled us to Himself through Christ and gave us the ministry of reconciliation: that God was reconciling the world to Himself in Christ, not counting people's sins against them. And He has committed to us the message of reconciliation. We are therefore Christ's ambassadors, as though God were making His appeal through us. We implore you on Christ's behalf: Be reconciled to God. God made Him who had no sin to be sin for us, so that in Him we might become the righteousness of God.

2 Corinthians 5:16-21 (NIV)

Leave your gift there in front of the altar. First go and be reconciled to them; then come and offer your gift.

Matthew 5:24 (NIV)

Overlook Offenses, and Go Above and Beyond What You Feel

This is imperative. You can't trust your feelings.

- **Off** with the old man. You are new, let your response glorify God.

> *A person's wisdom yields patience;*
> *it is to one's glory to overlook an offense.*
>
> Proverbs 19:11 (NIV)

Overlooking an offense and going beyond the pain that someone has caused gives us the opportunity to extend grace. Overlooking pain is not to ignore it or to pretend that it didn't happen, rather it enables us to view it from a higher position and see the full picture. We are able to see more than what that person has done and think about why they may have hurt us. Perhaps that person is going through a situation so awful that it caused their hurtful disposition.

Is your child experiencing pain or hurt that is causing her to offend others or you? An unhappy person, and this includes children, may cause others to be unhappy. You have heard it said that misery loves company. Stop, look down, and see the complete picture. Don't focus on what is directly in front of you.

Sometimes when others hurt us we put up our guard, and we fear opening up again. We protect ourselves from repeated pain.

No Perfect Parent, Just a Perfect Purpose

Often when others are abrupt and rude we chose to avoid them. But we can't love big by avoiding people.

Allow yourself to always love like you have never been hurt. Trust that God will heal you each time you experience heartbreak. I hold dear to what one of my favorite pastors expounds upon often, *Hurting people hurt people.* I must choose to see past the offense, knowing it is important to stop and realize that this person is likely in need of something, and this is what has caused them to hurt me. I must not take it personally. I must not stand in front of the attack but take a step to the side and realize that this is not about me.

Distance yourself from the pain, and ask yourself what this person needs and how you may help them? Let's make it simple. If someone hurts you, they must be hurting.

While writing this book God reminded me of a story that I was told when I was little, *The Lion and the Mouse.* After researching the story, I discovered that it is an old Aesop's fable told in many different ways.

The way that I heard this story was that the lion was mean and aggressive, and all of the animals feared him. He brooded and roared, scaring the other animals. But a teeny mouse chose to look past his own fears. He elected to not focus on the fears of being hurt or eaten.

And when the lion approached him, the mouse actually saw his pain and not his ferocious demeanor. The mouse saw that the lion had a thorn in his paw, causing him much distress and agony. This hurt caused the lion to be angry and unkind. The mouse mustered up the courage to pull out the thorn, and the lion yelled out in pain. Once the thorn was out of the lion's paw, he was grateful to the mouse and thanked him. After that the lion was kind and caring to all of the animals in the jungle.

This story touches me in so many ways. The mouse feared the lion but looked past his fear and rescued the lion. The mouse could have taken the safe route, as the other animals did, and ran away or avoided the lion. The bravery of the mouse improved the lives of all of the animals.

God wants us to see past our fears and walk in faith. He wants us not to get offended, hurt, or scared but rather to place the needs of others ahead of our own. The insight gained from this story is that the lion's encounter with love transformed him.

Since God has loved us in such a magnificent and abundant way, we need to be able to love others without fear. My love for others may transform more than their behavior, it may also transform their life.

My love should allow me to look beyond the fear and devise a courageous approach to meet the needs of others. It is the same courage displayed when a hero rushes into a burning building.

His love for people pushes aside his concern for himself and permits him to recuse those in need. When we refuse to fear, we are empowered to perform miracles. Let's all be heroes.

*Do nothing from selfish ambition or conceit,
but in humility count others more significant than yourselves.*

Philippians 2:3 (ESV)

There is no fear in love. But perfect love drives out fear, because fear has to do with punishment. The one who fears is not made perfect in love.

1 John 4:18 (NIV)

So do not fear, for I am with you; do not be dismayed, for I am your God. I will strengthen you and help you; I will uphold you with my righteous right hand.

Isaiah 41:10 (NIV)

Overlooking an offense allows us to win the victory of an attack launched by Satan! Someone being offensive and someone being offended are Satan's most effective and destructive weapons. Don't forget, Satan comes to steal, kill, and destroy. We cannot allow him to have his way. We must be aware of Satan's strategic plan to cause us to look at the offender who stands in front of us and not at the real enemy, whom we cannot see.

The weapon of *offense* is one of Satan's most destructive traps. Try contemplating each situation to determine if Satan is trying to *steal* your joy, *kill* your dream, or *destroy* your future. We cannot allow him any leeway in our life. We must recognize his strategy and not place blame on the offender who offended us. We must see Satan as the real enemy.

Offense is a personal attack because the enemy crafted it specifically for you. Satan uses everything he has learned about you, from when you were a baby to who you are now. He knows exactly who and how someone can best deliver the offending blow to us in order to be the most successful. That's right, he packaged the attack in the precise person to gain the biggest reaction and distraction to cause you to step away from who God called you to be.

Often it is someone who is closest to us who Satan will use to deliver the offense. It is important not to look at the person delivering the offense as the enemy. Maybe the reason that Satan was able to use him is because he is carrying around a hurt. Remember, *hurting people hurt people*, and our battle is not with flesh and blood.

When we focus on the facts and details of the offense and how it personally made us feel hurt, disrespected, and wronged, we can't focus on our purpose. You are on a mission to raise Godly children for His glory. Distraction shouldn't be an option.

For our struggle is not against flesh and blood, but against the rulers, against the authorities, against the powers of this dark world and against the spiritual forces of evil in the heavenly realms.

Ephesians 6:12 (NIV)

Be alert and of sober mind. Your enemy the devil prowls around like a roaring lion looking for someone to devour.

1 Peter 5:8 (NIV)

And the LORD's servant must not be quarrelsome but must be kind to everyone, able to teach, not resentful. Opponents must be gently instructed, in the hope that God will grant them repentance leading them to a knowledge of the truth, and that they will come to their senses and escape from the trap of the devil, who has taken them captive to do his will.

2 Timothy 2:24-26 (NIV)

> *Each of us should please our neighbors for their good, to build them up. For even Christ did not please Himself but, as it is written: "The insults of those who insult you have fallen on me." For everything that was written in the past was written to teach us, so that through the endurance taught in the Scriptures and the encouragement they provide we might have hope.*
>
> Romans 15:2-4 (NIV)

* * *

We, too, must have a strategic plan to overcome our trials. Let's focus on what is important.

Tell and show your children often that you love and value them. Give them lots of hugs and kisses. Read to them, and tell them bedtime stories. Create family rituals that express love, compassion, and empathy. Consistency in showing affection is just as important as any other area of parenting. In fact, I believe it is more so. Learn the way that your child best feels connected and loved. We all have a language of love that speaks to our hearts; know your child's.

Finding expressive ways to celebrate your child's accomplishments encourages more of them. Sharing in his disappointments with the same intensity as he feels them shows a profound manifestation of connection and empathy.

If your child has a rough day, replete with meltdowns and misunderstandings, let the night wash everything away by showing her unconditional love. Keep your child's works of art, and fashion a showcase for them that is more than the kitchen refrigerator. If possible, professionally frame a few pieces of her art work. If this is not possible, buy a nice frame. It is worth making this a budget priority.

If you can't afford to purchase a nice frame, check flea markets or garage sales. As a last resort, use recycled materials to make one. Find a prominent place to hang the art. It is *that* important. Showing that you value what your children have made articulates that you value the gifts inside of them.

Introduce new family traditions in partnership with your children. Do things to make them feel special, like the unique and extraordinary gift that they are to you and to the world.

Avoid favoritism at all cost. This is a spirit killer. Don't add that lifelong pain to your child's life. Your child was created for a greater purpose than she or you may be aware of now, but God will reveal it. Remind him that God has a magnificent purpose for his life. Knowing how to love is essential in living out our purpose. When we feel loved, we love better, stronger, and more.

* * *

I will praise thee; for I am fearfully and wonderfully made: marvelous are thy works; and that my soul knoweth right well.

Psalms 139:14

For He chose us in Him before the creation of the world to be holy and blameless in his sight. In love He predestined us for adoption to sonship through Jesus Christ, in accordance with His pleasure and will to the praise of His glorious grace, which He freely gives us in the One He loves.

Ephesians 1:2-6 (NIV)

Parents with infants and toddlers hear it all the time: before you realize it, your child will be all grown up. I am not sure if parents of toddlers can ever truly comprehend these words. But when an older mother rattles this off to you, take a moment to think back to when your baby was first born, and then gaze at him now. Time does move in the blink of an eye. Therefore, try as hard as you can to embrace every second as if it was a treasure providing spiritual growth and maturity wrapped in a precious package.

It is easy to become engrossed in all of the duties necessary to keep a household running or get swept up in the mundane chores of life. We sometimes miss things that we should notice. When your child is having a hard day, you need to be able to identify it and provide comfort. Maybe the comfort is as easy as making time to allow your child to rest in your lap. We all have ideas about how best to make a bad day feel better.

I used to keep inexpensive gifts on hand for tough days that needed a touch of happiness. It was my secret toy stash. I had bubbles, Hot Wheels, and trading cards with a few science gadgets thrown in. A dollar store goes a long way toward brightening a child's day.

Relief from a day gone awry doesn't have to cost anything. You could listen to your child's music or watch a movie with her. Quality time is a gift that makes most children happy from head to toe and ear to ear.

Our children have days when things go wrong. Tough times sometimes start at an early age.

We should give our children a resting place after the bumps and bruises of their day deplete them physically, mentally, or both. When your child is whinny, evaluate his needs, and respond in an appropriate way. Ponder if he needs you to stop and offer comfort. Be willing to put your child first when he needs you. Love is in our daily actions, not displayed only in providing necessary provisions.

Putting your child first can be challenging at times. It's not always simple to set aside your troubles and focus on your child. Below is another acronym to help walk you through some of the tough times when your bad day coincides with your child's. SIMPLE offers a way to redirect your focus and assist you in managing the overwhelming feelings of stress that you may be feeling.

Even if you can't recall all of the suggestions from the acronym SIMPLE, remembering a few is beneficial.

Stop and pray.

Imagine the rest of the day as perfect. Why? Because this produces gratefulness and optimism.

Move to a state of happiness. This is a choice.

And now, brothers, as I close this letter, let me say this one more thing: Fix your thoughts on what is true and good and right. Think about things that are pure and lovely, and dwell on the fine, good things in others. Think about all you can praise God for and be glad about.

Philippians 4:8 (TLB)

Praise. Sing a song to the Lord. Speak out loud words of gratitude to the Lord.

Laugh. Find something to laugh about. You or your child can tell a joke, tickle each other, or be silly. Laugh!

Then our mouth was filled with laughter, and our tongue with singing. Then they said among the nations, "The Lord has done great things for them."

Psalms 126:2

Encourage yourself and your child. Invoke all of the scriptures that you have memorized to encourage and strengthen yourself and your child. When nothing else is working, encourage yourself in the Lord. Do it with the word of God.

Be assured, if you walk with Him and look to Him,
and expect help from Him, He will never fail you.
— George Mueller, Evangelist

And David was greatly distressed;
for the people spake of stoning him, because the soul of all the
people was grieved, every man for his sons and for his daughters:
but David encouraged himself in the Lord *his God.*

1 Samuel 30:6

We love because He first loved us.

1 John 4:19 (BLB)

RECAP

- Use NITRO:

  Never give up

  Interrupt negative thoughts with positive ones

  Trust God

  Reconciliation

  Overlook offenses.

- Show no favoritism, and give each child one-on-one time.

- Use your child's love language.

- Use SIMPLE:

  Stop and pray

  Imagine the rest of the day as perfect

  Move to a state of happiness

  Praise

  Laugh

  Encourage yourself and your child.

CHAPTER SIX

Embrace the Power of Play

An enormous amount of research supports the view that play has massive benefits for all living animals. The more intellectual an animal is, the greater the need for play. Animals that display compound reasoning skills add more complexity to their play. Play has the capacity to move us into a state of happiness, relaxation, and calmness. It may also provide us with an adrenaline rush, exhilaration, and thrills. It is instrumental in generating a passion for life and learning.

I think that Diane Ackman, poet and author, articulates it best, *Play is our brain's favorite way of learning.* Play motivates us to exercise and move, which improves the blood flow to our brains. Play also cultivates strong bonds in relationships. It is a phenomenal way to improve logical thinking skills and increase brain plasticity. Brain plasticity is also called neuroplasticity and is the ability of the brain to adapt its connections or rewire itself.

This is important because it allows us to continue learning as we age or use other parts of our brain if one part of it becomes damaged.

Play used in every area of our lives makes them more fulfilling. When I was an enrichment director in elementary schools, I noticed that most children in kindergarten were excited about school. But as they got older, many second and third grade students disengaged. School became a burden, and the joys of learning no longer existed for them. This was particularly distressing to me because I had seen what happened to students who gave up on school.

At that time my family and I were living in a community that had been nicknamed Mont Ghetto. Gangs, shootings, and killings were common in this neighborhood. I had grown up in this community, and even though the community had changed, I wasn't fearful living there. It was my home.

I did, however, feel a nagging ache because so many children were going to jail or dying. I was aware that part of the reason why this was happening was due to the lack of hope. I also understood that children who did well in school had a genuine sense of hope. So I felt a strong responsibility to make sure that my son's passion for learning never died. And that is why I sought out the power of play.

This started out as a strategy to advance the interests of my own son that quickly became a way to help all children. I have always recognized that play revives the soul. Then, after learning about the importance of play from many child development classes, books, workshops, and seminars, it enthralled me.

I began to witness the amazing results of learning through play, both as a mother and as an enrichment director. I was fascinated with how play could re-energize the weary. It consoled those who were sad, it could relieve those who were stressed, it could even inspire innovation, determination, and creativity. One's imagination was the limit!

As a result, early in my children's lives I endorsed learning through play. I encouraged and supported their play with resources, equipment, and time. With their grandiose dreams in full throttle, we went in whatever direction that play took us. When my son announced at the age of four that he was going to be a chef, I bought him a kid kitchen, found lots of fun recipe books, and we cooked almost daily.

When he changed his career goals at age eight to wanting to be a marine biologist, I painted an ocean mural on his wall and bought him an aquarium and a chemistry set. My commitment to play was serious. He changed his career goals many times, but each hour of play took him closer to his purpose. He ended up being a surgeon! Who knew? God!

My daughter played her way to becoming a computer engineer in a classified position. But before college she announced at the age of five that she would be a school teacher. As a mother dedicated to play, I bought her a chalkboard, lots of stackable chairs from the flea market, and we fashioned a classroom and a library in our home. Armed with more imagination than money, we made stuff, we found things, and we pretended that we had what we needed!

Play is a remarkable catalyst to pointing people to their purpose. I encouraged and motivated children to excel by using something that is intrinsic to them, play. I incorporated different themes to cover a variety of interests. Each theme inspired each child differently, however, the achievement was always the same.

Experiencing such overall success with my children, my nieces and nephew, and my school students, I started a business specializing in the benefits of play. This was a difficult decision because I was fearful of leaving what I thought was secure employment. Also, I wasn't confident that I was the right person to promote play.

In the midst of my struggle with birthing my business, I decided to include play in a ministry for the homeless at my mom's church. I had been working alongside my mother for eight years feeding the homeless, being responsible for decorating, setting the tables, and serving. This was a job into which I sometimes felt I didn't invest enough thought.

Since play was my ministry, one day I decided to go all-out and place colorful mini mind puzzles on our hot pink and electric teal decorated tables. Not knowing what to expect, I observed something amazing.

First, the pastor of the church, who hadn't gotten more than a couple hours of sleep the previous night, trudged in as if he carried the weight of the world on his shoulders. His lack of sleep was obvious, with his bloodshot eyes and his eyelids puffy and droopy like a wilting sunflower at the end of a long hot season.

He made his way to the tables near the wall. He eased himself onto the hard metal chair that I had set out earlier. He rested his head against the brick wall and took several long, drawn-out breaths.

But he noticed one of the puzzles on the table. He picked it up and tried to solve it. He shook it one way and then another. He twisted his face from side to side, almost in an effort to help manipulate the ball to where he wanted it to go. He smiled with each small accomplishment. He was playing! First one ball and then another fell into place, and when he had gotten all the balls in place, he beamed. In fact, I think I heard him giggle.

He set the puzzle down with the most pleased expression I had seen from him that entire day. Even though his eyes were still crimson and his body language still hollered exhaustion, his countenance was peaceful. He glanced down the table and discovered another puzzle. Suddenly, his attention was drawn to the homeless people traipsing down the stairs to be fed.

He bowed his head as he greeted them but didn't stand up as he did most days. As soon as the group of ten to 12 homeless people had settled in at the tables, we served them drinks. The pastor's focus went immediately back to the puzzle that he had noticed down the table from him. I had placed three sets of five different puzzles in a bowl on each table.

He didn't stop at one, he did all five.

The homeless people, who appeared beaten down from life, savored their drinks. Some in the group spoke English well, some were black, some were white, and most of them were men. These men showed up on most Saturdays, so we knew them well. They trekked 15 blocks just to get to the church.

They were serious and generally didn't talk much. Their hands were dirty, their clothes stained, and their hair unkempt, as you would expect from those living on the street. Some smelled of alcohol, others emitted the scent of weed, some reeked of the streets on which they lived. As usual, their faces were weary, and their body language exuded defeat. They were there to eat.

One of our regulars dropped his head and noticed one of the bowls of puzzles on the table. He took a puzzle from the bowl.

He smiled, squealed, and then persuaded the others to try. Then they all had puzzles! They all played!

Their bodies relaxed, and their faces brightened. They chuckled, and some playfully jeered at the others. Some were quiet and intent but still seemed at ease.

Their food was soon ready, and we placed their home-cooked, Southern-style, hot-from-the-kitchen, cooked-with-love meals on the table in front of them. But they refused to put their puzzles down. Almost as if surprised by his own actions, one mentioned to the others that their food was getting cold. They laughed but continued to play. One by one they solved their puzzles, which gave them permission to eat their food.

Now, our homeless people were always grateful, always appreciative, and always polite. They never stole from us and always inquired if they could take things set on the tables that we intended for them to take. Whether it was food or little gifts like Bibles, they always made a point to get permission to keep whatever it was. To my astonishment, when the people left, they took my puzzles. They did not check to see if this was okay, and their hands were empty, leaving me to suppose that they snuck my puzzles into their pockets or backpacks.

They did, however, leave me with many questions. The whole purpose of the homeless people being there was to get a hot, home-cooked meal. Meals for them didn't come every day, and we served them just twice a month, but only if they could endure the long hike to get there.

I was curious about why they had played the way they had. I wanted to understand why they took my puzzles. And why did the pastor spend his rest time playing with puzzles? What compelled these folks to play?

Food is essential for life, but is play? The biggest question I had was, *What does God think about play?* The answer to this question was imperative to me because I was launching a business centered around the benefits of play.

I so deeply wanted to comprehend what God thought that I researched the subject. I searched the Bible, questioned a few pastors and theologians, and checked the Internet. But I really didn't find an answer.

I read a book called *Play: How it Shapes the Brain*, by Dr. Stuart Brown, and concluded that, yes, play is vital and not just for children. But one question plagued me even more, *What does God think?* I secretly worried that God didn't approve of play for adults. Therefore, how could it be needed to survive?

How I was raised as a child and possibly these scriptures somehow influenced my beliefs that God didn't like play.

When I was a child, I spake as a child, I understood as a child, I thought as a child: but when I became a man, I put away childish things.

1 Corinthians 13:11

Neither be ye idolaters, as were some of them; as it is written, "The people sat down to eat and drink, and rose up to play."

1 Corinthians 10:7

Neither filthiness, nor foolish talking, nor jesting, which are not convenient: but rather giving of thanks.

Ephesians 5:4

I always associated play for adults with *lazy*, and I knew that God didn't like lazy. Words like *stop playing around* were words that I never wanted directed at me. I am a hard worker, and I think that everyone should be. God is clear that we all should work.

His LORD answered and said unto him, "Thou wicked and slothful servant, thou knewest that I reap where I sowed not, and gather where I have not strawed."

Matthew 25:26

> *The way of the slothful man is as a hedge of thorns, but the way of the righteous is made plain.*
>
> Proverbs 15:19

> *That ye be not slothful, but followers of them who through faith and patience inherit the promises.*
>
> Hebrews 6:12

The tone of these scriptures throughout the Bible caused me grief. As the concern about God's disapproval was becoming troublesome, I read the last chapter of *Play: How it Shapes the Brain* and had an epiphany. It was my personal discovery about play.

God whispered to me, *Play is not play, it is practice.* I was looking for the wrong word. *What does God think about practice?*

Practice was the seed that God planted within all of us to accomplish our purpose. Through play we are practicing life and gathering the stuff needed to succeed in our own life journey. God gave us the gift of joy in practicing the skills that transport us to our purpose. The joy in practicing is called *play*!

Equipped with this information, things became clear. I understood that the pastor and the homeless people were practicing handling the twists and turns in life situations that they would encounter with humor, ingenuity, and smarts. God was keeping their skills sharp.

The same thing is true of a football player and all of the preparation that goes into playing a game. A college athlete who plays football is merely practicing the skills that God wants to develop within him. This practice teaches him perseverance, how to follow the rules, to be on time, and how to work hard, the skills that God wants His children to acquire for their life purpose. Don't look at the activity, rather see the skills developed through play.

My son learned at an early age to serve people with the career goal of becoming a chef. He learned about mixing up different chemicals with the goal of saving a life, which made him happy with a career goal as a marine biologist. And his play led him ultimately to his life purpose of serving people with compassion and his tremendous medical skills as a surgeon.

I have heard it described as a *play profile*. I might describe it more as a *practice profile*, as life's guide to your purpose. I believe that *the purpose that God has assigned to each of us will be revealed in each detailed accomplishment of play.*

The questions is, *Does God like practice?* The answer is that God loves us to practice what is good!

Little children, don't let anyone deceive you. The person who practices righteousness is righteous, just as the Messiah is righteous.

1 John 3:7 (ISV)

What you have learned and received and heard and seen in me, practice these things, and the God of peace will be with you.

Philippians 4:9 (ESV)

I have included for you here some important research information about play. It is easy to dismiss its unassuming power. Understanding its value helps us comprehend how remarkable this gift is that God has given us.

Facts About Play

- Improves memory and stimulates the growth of the cerebral cortex (Diamond, et al).

- Increases attention to detail and focus (Pellegrini and Holmes, 2006).

- Activates the brain's reward circuitry while reducing stress (Bloomsbury USA, 2011. One World Publications, 2011).

- Improves employee morale and increases productivity (Gallup Press, 2010).

- Increases employee retention (Penn State, Loyola University of Maryland, and Ohio State University, team study).

- Produces innovative thinking and creativity (Russ Johnson, *Play: The New Leadership Secret That Changes Everything*, 2014).

One adage that I like is, *When you learn with stress you retain less. When you learn with play the message will stay.*

You can include play in most areas of your child's life. I have provided for you below a few suggestions that will help you to make play readily available for your child.

- Leave a puzzle on the family room table or in a place where the entire family may come together throughout the week to complete it. This offers the opportunity to strengthen family bonds and for family members to work together and communicate.

- Make a to-go play bag using a pencil pouch, and fill it with crayons, pencils, note pads, play dough, and bubbles. Use your resourcefulness. Encourage kids to play with the play bag instead of the iPad. This will help inspire your child's creativity rather than depending on the imaginations of the designers of game apps. It also will strengthen hands-on application skills.

- Keep an engaging storybook in the car or in your purse to read to your child if you have waiting times. This will help develop listening skills, focus, and the ability to dream.

- Plan a play date with your child once a month. This will compel you to go somewhere designed for children. Consider the children's museum, an arcade, or somewhere else special to him. This reminds him of how important he is to you, thereby increasing his self-esteem. It will also help you recognize the gifts hidden within so that you may build on your child's play patterns.

- Try some whimsical play, such as camping in the living room or building a Tootsie Roll log cabin. Release your thoughts to soar with fun ideas. Keep in mind, you are building skills for a purpose. Children who play with their parents develop strong verbal communication skills, feel a stronger sense of connection, and are more confident in who they are.

- Spell the words on your child's spelling list using glitter, or use scented markers to fashion fun flash cards. Have them make two sets of cards, and play a matching game.

This allows them to practice writing and recognizing the words, all for the joy of play. Be innovative. Make learning fun, and your child will retain so much more.

- Limit screen time. Instead, encourage hands-on, interactive play. Add Legos® and other building toys to your child's toy collection. These kinds of toys inspire inventive thinking and creativity. Board games increase concentration and help children learn to take turns, along with many other benefits.

Below is your acronym for PLAY. Resolve to appreciate and retain this one. It will change your life.

Purposeful

Living

Advances

You

God has equipped each of us with what I call a Michael Jordan talent. No, I am not suggesting that everyone has the ability to score 40 points a game and dunk a basketball by age 16. But I am confident that your child enjoys something that she could do for hours. What is it? What drives your child to this activity? Your child's talent is revealed in her play, it's her passion.

Maybe this activity makes him happy, perhaps time stops when he is engaged in this activity. Helping your child discover his talent isn't always as easy as you might think. Often the talent doesn't present itself without children having many different and unique opportunities to try new things. God has gifted each of us with an incredible talent. Explore what your child is passionate about, and partner with him to develop that interest.

If you can't figure out your purpose, figure out your passion. For your passion will lead you right into your purpose.
— T.D. Jakes, Pastor, Author, and Filmmaker

Michael Jordan was actually cut from his charter high school basketball team. His story is that he worked hard and made an awesome comeback. His love for basketball allowed him to work relentlessly to become better. He practiced long hours. Time disappeared when he practiced, and his talent reached superiority. Greatness is developed, but we are given natural talents that grow larger than life when we practice them.

Passion and Purpose Offer Provision

Ralph Waldo Emerson professed, *It is a happy talent to know how to play.* This is true because in our play our gifts are made visible. Take notice of your child, and understand what gifts are being revealed through her play. Nourish those gifts. Your child's purpose lies within those gifts.

It is important to make time for your child to play and for you to play with him. Time for play needs to be in the daily schedule. It is *that* critical to raising greatness. Incorporating the power of play into our lives allows us to prosper in many ways. Enjoy it, and see what God is preparing your child for with His gift of play.

Children need the freedom and time to play. Play is not a luxury. Play is a necessity.

— Kay Redfield Jamison, Clinical Psychologist

Play is the work of childhood.

— Jean Piaget

Sometimes you have to play a long time to be able to play like yourself.

— Miles Davis

> *It is becoming increasingly clear through research on the brain, as well as in other areas of study, that childhood needs play. Play acts as a forward feed mechanism into courageous, creative, rigorous thinking in adulthood.*
> — Tina Bruce, Professor and Play Theorist

> *Play is the only way the highest intelligence of humankind can unfold.*
> — Joseph Chilton Pearce,
> Professor of Child and Human Development

Play is not just for your children. Take a moment and reminisce about when you were a young child, how you loved to play. Play can still bring you happiness and refresh your soul. It is important to take time to play. You need it. Parenting isn't easy. Play has powerful benefits that help relieve stress and ignite a passion for life. Find time to nurture your inner self with play.

Your purpose is also in your play. When you live in your purpose, it advances you to unlimited opportunities, such as joy, success, and peace. Always make time to PLAY.

Adult play could include gardening, cooking, or many other things that allow you to be creative and express a passion. It could be hiking, biking, or playing an instrument. Your play is unique to you, designed by the master giver of gifts. *Every good and perfect gift comes from above.* (James 1:17)

> *Play keeps us vital and alive.*
> *It gives us an enthusiasm for life that is irreplaceable.*
> *Without it, life just doesn't taste good.*
>
> — Lucia Capocchione, Art Therapist

RECAP

- Incorporate PLAY into life's challenges.

- Invest time, money, and thought into **PLAY**. It pays you back.

- Use PLAY:

    Purposeful

    Living

    Advances

    You.

    This is true in all areas of your life.

CHAPTER SEVEN

Ducks, Eagles, and Naysayers

Don't let the naysayers change the way you do things. If God said to do it, get it done. Many times, my parenting approach was questioned. Sometimes it was insulted. One mom I knew stated that I was too much of an authoritarian and that my children would grow up, and in her words, *go crazy and butt wild*.

She had an older child whom she insisted went off the deep end because of too many rules when he was young. Now she was heartbroken because he had chosen an unhealthy lifestyle that included drugs and rebellious living. She advised me sternly to relax my rules and expectations for my children. She did this as an older mom who didn't want me to experience her pain.

She had noble intentions. I appreciated her advice and prayed for guidance. And I stood on the fact that my family would continue to have rules and expectations in my household.

When my children were young I expected them to follow my rules, or there would be definite consequences. I did not spare the rod. I will share my thoughts about discipline in the next chapter. I think that others often saw the solitude of my children and thought that it was generated from a dictatorship parenting style.

As I mentioned before, intentional parenting allows your children to grow and make responsible decisions for themselves. I did undeniably try to help my children navigate the challenges of life. But I did less of that the older they became.

Peer pressure is hard for children to stand up against. They need something to combat our natural tendency to be part of the group at all cost. We had a motto in our house: *Do you want to be a duck or an eagle?* Ducks waddle along following each other, but an eagle soars alone. But I almost stopped using this motto for two reasons. First, it sounds harsh. Second, I met a lady who challenged me with information about eagles that I didn't know.

She alleged that eagles are a prideful and unwise bird. Wow! She had done some research and discovered that an eagle would drown rather than let go of a fish four times its weight. The eagle would fight to its end to kill its prey instead of letting it go and finding something that it could easier manage.

But God dropped this nugget into my spirit. The majestic eagle is not prideful, rather it will die fulfilling its purpose, which is to hunt.

And we know many people who died for their purpose. Both Martin Luther King Jr. and Jesus died fulfilling their purpose. In fact, below are listed five valuable attributes about the eagle that hide extraordinary wisdom:

- Eagles have keen vision. We, too, can have excellent vision that will permit us to prosper in life.
- Eagles are powerful. Each of us has a power within that will help us accomplish the impossible.
- Eagles are determined. They are known to kill prey up to three times their size. If their prey fights, eagles fight harder. They don't give up. Grab hold of this and live by it.
- Eagles soar high. They don't fly away from storms but are confident in their strength. Eagles use the updrafts in strong winds to conserve energy and flap their wings less. They soar. They rest in the storm and use a force more powerful than themselves to continue in their purpose. There is excellent wisdom in this for us. In the middle of a storm, rest, and trust the power greater than yourself.

- Eagles only eat live food. I love this. Words are nourishment to all souls. If the words of others are not alive with truth and goodness, don't eat them. They're not meant for consumption. Let this rest within your being that the word of God is living and active and should be consumed daily.

And to obtain incredible results, you may sometimes stand alone, but that isn't a bad thing. The motto of living as an eagle may sound as if I was training my children to live unconnected, but that was far from my goal. My objective of having my kids live like an eagle allowed them to be confident. If no one else wanted to do what they chose to do, it was still a good option.

If any choice is based first on God's word, sound judgment, and concern for others and yourself and is then not received, fly by yourself. Be an eagle.

Teaching children to not follow the crowd is important. Show them early that they can make wise choices for their life and that it isn't prudent to permit someone else to decide what is best for them. Help them understand that it is okay to be alone sometimes and to find joy in spending time by themselves. Support your child in cultivating quiet times that are fulfilling.

Some children learn a zealous appreciation for reading, others like drawing or building with Legos˚. Whatever the choice, it teaches children to be comfortable being alone. We also hear God better in our quiet times.

I recall once, when Nicole was 15, she wanted to go to a rave concert that I wasn't comfortable allowing her to attend. I had an uneasy feeling about the crowd, but I couldn't vocalize my concern. I prayed, and God instructed me to tell her to seek His permission. She strolled into the kitchen to convince me to let her go.

"Check with God." I didn't mince my words.

She stood there in utter disbelief and confusion. Then, all of a sudden, a happy smile spread across her face.

This doesn't look good. I clenched my teeth.

Before Nicole could turn around to go upstairs and have that conversation with God, I prayed. I watched her virtually dance up the stairs. God calmed me down, and I continued cooking dinner.

Twenty-five minutes later Nicole plodded back into the kitchen. She appeared dejected, as if she was going to cry. She told me that she couldn't go, that God had answered no.

I must be a horrible mom because my first thought was not to console my sweet girl, it was to sing with joy. I didn't sing, but it caught me by surprise that God would answer her so promptly and that I was so worried for no reason.

She got over it and stayed in the kitchen and helped me finish cooking dinner. We chatted, giggled, and talked about all kinds of silly stuff. And then I grew bold enough to ask her how God spoke to her and how she knew it was God.

"Mom," she spoke matter-of-factly, "I checked into all of the details and found out that I'm not even old enough. I would have had to lie to get in. That's how I knew God's answer was no."

This was a lesson of trust for me. If God tells you to do something, do it. Don't delay. My obedience offered Nicole an opportunity to have a God interaction and kept me from being the bearer of bad news.

Every child is different. That is the glorious thing about all of us. We are all formed for God's perfect purpose. He identifies what we need so much better than anyone else. If God tells you what is best for your child, it is up to you to decide that He is right and obey without delay.

> *He replied, "Blessed rather are those*
> *who hear the word of God and obey it."*
> Luke 11:28 (NIV)

I often sought advice because I knew enough to realize that I didn't have all the answers. There were also times when I received unsolicited advice, which can be fruitful. However, you also need to be careful. The secret is in discerning what to do with the advice because some of it is meant to be used, and some is meant to be stepped on to make you taller.

Advice will come, so be prepared. Many times I learned from Kenneth's experiences, and Nicole reaped the benefits.

When Kenneth was 16 years old, I took him to the pediatrician for his wellness check. When the nurse called his name, I didn't move but remained seated in the lobby. *Maybe Kenneth is getting to an age where he might not want me in the room with him and his doctor.*

He stood and looked at me. "Mom, what's wrong? You're going with me, right?"

Pulling Kenneth close to me, I whispered, "It's okay if you want to go by yourself. You are getting older. Don't you want your privacy?"

"Come on, Mom. Let's go." Kenneth pulled me up by my arm.

His doctor had been at the hospital when he was born. She was our family doctor and had also seen my baby brother for years. She had seen Kenneth for regular check-ups and minor illnesses over the years, but now he had become a teenager.

She began with a series of rather benign questions and progressed to some offensive ones. Don't get me wrong. It is important for the doctor to have all of the information needed to address personal issues, but it isn't okay to push when the answer has already been clearly stated.

"Are you having sex?" Dr. Shanuti continued the grilling.

"No."

She raised her eyebrows, frowned, and requested that I wait outside. I grabbed my purse, stood, and took a few steps toward the door.

Kenneth spoke up. "Mom, don't leave. I want you here."

I turned back and sat.

Dr. Shanuti peered at Kenneth. "Is that answer for your mom's benefit, since she is here in the room with us?"

"No." Kenneth was visibly agitated.

Her statement seemed to bother him. I wasn't sure how to respond.

Dr. Shanuti inquired further, "Do you even like girls? Do you find girls attractive? Do you notice your body reacting to them in ways that you may not have noticed in the past?"

"I like girls." Embarrassed, Kenneth shrugged.

"But you have never had a sexual encounter with a girl?"

Kenneth didn't open his mouth but stared at the doctor in disbelief.

She rattled off questions without pausing long enough for Kenneth to answer them. "Are you gay? It is quite uncommon for someone of your age not to have had some type of sexual encounter. Do I need to provide you with protection? There is no shame in being gay. I see hundreds of normal teens each year that are sexually active. Do you really expect me to believe that you will not have sex within the next year? Do you feel comfortable expressing how you feel about sex? Okay, do you have any questions that I can answer for you?

"Do you think your son is being honest? I believe that he may be trying to hide the truth from you," Dr. Shanuti turned her head in my direction.

"I am not gay! Didn't you hear me! I like girls. One day I will marry one of them and have sex. Enough said!" Kenneth lost his patience.

Looking back, I was ill-prepared for this attack on my son. Dr. Shanuti didn't know that God had a purpose for this child, whom I was raising for greatness, but I did.

God had Kenneth in a place to not feel pressured to act like the rest of the teens in our culture to whom the doctor referred to as *normal*. He was committed to waiting until marriage.

I wish that I had been more of an advocate for Kenneth in the doctor's office when she implied that my son must be gay or that he was trying to keep me in the dark because he really was having sex at 16.

Dr Shanuti snarled, "Mothers think that they know their children, but they act differently when Mom and Dad aren't around. At his age, it is unlikely that he is still a virgin."

I didn't listen to the inner voice talking to my spirit. I wanted to stand up to her and tell her that I was confident that Kenneth was being truthful and to mind her own business. I was afraid because of all of her years of higher education and experience. I was sure that she had to know what she was doing.

Kenneth glared at Dr. Shanuti, but he did not say another word. He had to speak up for himself that day, and he did an awesome job. Why? He knew how to soar like an eagle even when his mom waddled like a duck.

Kenneth had two girlfriends in college before he married his third and, ultimately, the best one for him. This confirmed for me, if I needed confirmation, that the doctor didn't understand God's plan. The doctor's inquisition that day helped me stand taller next time.

Eight years later, Nicole reached the age of 14 and the time of her appointment with Dr. Shanuti. Dr. Shanuti started in right away telling me that Nicole was now at the age where she would be sexually active.

She shook her finger at me and cautioned me. "You got lucky with that son of yours. He is definitely a one-in-a-million kid. That said, I don't want you to have unrealistic expectations for a teenage girl in this day and age. The cultural norm around sex has gotten much more relaxed. Besides, your son was here almost ten years ago. Right?"

"Trust me. You won't be so lucky this time. I am never wrong twice. How about you step into the hall for a moment while Nicole and I chat?"

I believe that in her mind, she felt that she was being an advocate for my daughter. She was wrong again, and she was also the one not so lucky that day. I had learned from the previous experience with my son, and Nicole was about to reap the rewards of me standing taller.

"I would like my mother to stay in the room, and I would like you to know that my mother lets me make my own choices. Furthermore, dating isn't that important at my age." Before I spoke up, Nicole did.

Dr. Shanuti paused before launching into her spiel. "It's only normal to want to have intimacy in relationships. When do you plan on becoming sexually active? After all, this is 2008! I'm sure that a pretty girl like you is dating, even if Mom doesn't know about it yet. Am I right?"

And then it was my turn to speak up.

I verbalized my expectations. "It is not your job to determine when Nicole will develop an intimate relationship or have sex. You will not bombard my daughter with a host of questions that she has already answered. My parenting spoke for itself with Kenneth. I want you to focus on the physical aspects of my daughter's health and nothing more. I will handle the rest. If this is a problem, we can find a new doctor."

The saddest part about this was that Dr. Shanuti was aware of my belief that unless one is contemplating getting married, there is no reason to date. Knowing this, she still pushed and questioned my values in front of my children and offered her advice. She made accusations about the integrity of my children by suggesting that they were lying. She questioned their character by stating that all children engage in sexual exploration at their age and that if they don't, something is wrong with them.

She insulted my parenting and my awareness while insisting that it was unreasonable to expect teenagers in the 1990s and 2000s to abstain. She voiced that it was poor judgement not to encourage them to use contraceptives. This was a well-respected doctor with many years of experience and accolades. She was at my bedside at the time of my children's births. Yet, I had never established boundaries for her giving me advice.

This is when I should have focused on the word that God had given me and not been shaken. I should have stood tall and spoken up first with Kenneth and sooner with Nicole.

God guided me to impart my beliefs early with my children about dating and to pray for their understanding as to why I wanted that for them. When they were toddlers, I told them that dating is for the purpose of finding a wife or a husband.

I started this early. We had discussions as to why this was so important, and I shared what I believed the Bible instructs about this subject. Not dating wasn't a mandate imposed by me. I revealed that it was my hope for their lives that they would wait. They had a choice, and they knew it.

You cannot mandate integrity or character, it must be developed. I can't impose my beliefs on my children, they must see the value in those beliefs for themselves.

I realized as a parent that if they had a relationship with a God who loved them, they would want to please Him even more than they wanted to please me. I don't have to be with them for them to make wise choices. Their choices reflected their own beliefs about a God who is always with them.

> *Love the LORD your God and keep His requirements,*
> *His decrees, His laws, and His commands always.*
> Deuteronomy 11:1 (NIV)

Sometimes the naysayers come into matters in our life unassuming. They may have views that they never thought much about. I perceived what some parents felt to be innocent behavior as dangerous.

One mom announced in an adoring tone, "Look at his little girlfriend. Aren't they a cute couple?"

She was referring to her five-year-old son and a five-year-old doll-like girl with whom he was playing for the day. Why put that into a young child's spirit? Peer pressure will spring up soon enough. Why make it seem like kids need to have a girlfriend or a boyfriend to be cute? And, as a parent, why would you make your child feel like you gain some pleasure in connecting them to someone else, especially so early?

I always put a halt to such talk when well-meaning parents voiced things like that about my son or daughter. I expressed my view that when he or she was ready to get married and God provided His vision to them, they would be ready to have a girlfriend or a boyfriend. I always ended the discussion by declaring that what we see now is two babies playing, nothing more.

Things become more alarming at school with children ten and 11 years old. I saw elementary school children overwhelmed with rejection from their boyfriend or girlfriend and have trouble coping. I saw kids' grades drop, fights, and the beginnings of eating disorders because someone's girlfriend or boyfriend broke up with them. These children needed to be concentrating on reading, math, and all of the benefits of school.

This is why intentional parenting requires us to think of the seemingly innocent behaviors that we adopt from the *now* culture and filter them through the word of God.

Do not love the world or anything in the world. If anyone loves the world, love for the Father is not in them.

1 John 2:15 (NIV)

Do not conform to the pattern of this world, but be transformed by the renewing of your mind. Then you will be able to test and approve what God's will is—His good, pleasing and perfect will.

Romans 12:2 (NIV)

Parents frequently receive lots of advice from so-called experts telling them the importance of talking to their children early about the dangerous world. They encourage discussions with adolescents about sex, online predators, and drugs. I feel that today, more than ever, before that discussion takes place we must help our kids develop the skills to problem-solve and discern the difference between good and evil. They need a keen awareness of the dreadfulness in the world and a practical plan to stay safe. This is vital.

No Perfect Parent, Just a Perfect Purpose

I chose to share with my children early in their lives information about potential dangers. We examined examples of those who took drugs, those who were promiscuous, or those struggling with other issues and discussed how this had negatively impacted their lives. We compared the lives of what they considered successful people and analyzed their habits.

I encouraged my children to seek God while I imparted my insight and experiences. They did not live in fear. They lived in the trust of God and in the good sense that He gave them first. This better equipped them to stand up for what they believed in.

I never gave my children curfews, though in the State of Colorado the law dictates curfews for teenagers. Of course, it was the kids' responsibility to follow the law. You may have noticed that I stated that meeting the state-mandated curfew was my children's responsibility because I trusted that they could handle it.

Now technology has thrown out even more ways for children to become ensnared in treacherous situations. They must be trained early that not all people whom they encounter have their well-being in mind. They must be able to stand on the word of God to traverse all of the challenges facing them.

I gave my children information about child molesters, gangs, terrorists, and violence targeted against children. This frightened them at times, but we collaborated regarding ways to be safe. Sometimes children comprehend situations that pose a threat to their safety that maybe parents are not aware of. Our open communication permits us to help our kids come up with solutions to their concerns and keep them safe.

Cultivating a strong and caring relationship was monumental in being able to speak to my children. I prayed for them and with them, and together we proved the naysayers wrong. We demonstrated how God answered and guided us through our prayers. Our daily testimonies brought us even closer together.

The pessimists will show up in different ways, sometimes well-educated and sometimes with the world as their focus. It is important to never forget that we need help to raise our children, but what God commands should always be the final word. Don't be too hard on yourself. You only answer to God, a God who gives grace freely.

When we delay in responding to what God tells us to do, it is disobedience. When you perceive that God has given you a clear word, do not let others influence you with their recommendation. They are trying to persuade you to do something different. Even though they may have your best interests in mind, it will not turn out well. The information that someone else divulges to you may seem wise in the eyes of the world.

Stay focused. Resolve to do what God tells you to do. Move on. Count it DONE.

- **Decide** that you will do what God put on your heart to do. Ignore the people who don't encourage you to be obedient to God.

- **Obey** God. Don't delay. Do what God tells you immediately, and don't allow people to contradict what you know God told you to do.

- **Never** stop believing. People and circumstances may cause you to want to change directions, but trust that God's advice is always the right choice.

- **Enjoy** and rest in the fact that when God tells you something and you obey Him, He has a blessing in store.

*He replied, "Blessed rather are those
who hear the word of God and obey it."*

Luke 11:28 (NIV)

And Samuel said, "Has the Lord as great delight in burnt offerings and sacrifices, as in obeying the voice of the Lord? Behold, to obey is better than sacrifice, and to listen than the fat of rams.

1 Samuel 15:22 (ESV)

For as by the one man's disobedience the many were made sinners, so by the one man's obedience the many will be made righteous.

Romans 5:19 (ESV)

I only gave them this command: "Obey me and I will be your God, and you will be my people. Do all that I command, and good things will happen to you."

Jeremiah 7:23 (ETR)

RECAP

- Use DONE:

    Decide that you will do what God puts on your heart to do

    Obey God

    Never stop believing

    Enjoy.

CHAPTER EIGHT

The Secret Gift

I suggest that before discipline starts, we need to discuss the fundamentals when it comes to a misbehaving child. Children's basic requirements must be met before certain expectations should be made of them. Make sure that your kids are sleeping enough. Children need sleep.

The lack of sleep may make most of us grumpy. My heart hurts when I see a tired child trying to function on a lack of sleep, yet he is expected to behave as if he is well rested. I think that this is a failure on the part of the parents. I understand that sometimes things happen in our schedules and that children can't get the sleep that they need. If your child didn't get the requisite amount of sleep, please give him the patience that he deserves!

Another basic influence on behavior is food. Is your child hungry? Are you offering healthy snacks when appropriate? A new term making the rounds today is *hangry*. This is a combi-

Recommended Amount of Sleep for Pediatric Populations*	
Age	Recommended Sleep Hours per 24 Hour Period
Infants: 4 to 12 months	12 to 16 hours (including naps)
Toddlers: 1 to 2 years	11 to 14 hours (including naps)
Preschoolers: 3 to 5 years	10 to 13 hours (including naps)
Gradeschoolers: 6 to 12 years	9 to 12 hours
Teens: 13 to 18 years	8 to 10 hours

*American academy of pediatrics (AAP) has issued a Statement of Endorsement supporting these guidelines from the American Academy of Sleep Medicine (AASM).

Source: Paruthi S. Brooks, LI, D'Ambrosia C, Hall W, Kotagal S., Lloyd RM, Malow B. Maski K, Nichols C, Quan SF, Rosen CL, Troester MM, Wse MS. Recommended Amount of Sleep forPediatric Populations: A Statement of the American Academy of Sleep Medicine. J clin Sleep used 2016 May 25. piii: jc-00158-16. PubMed PMID: 27250809.

nation of *hungry* and *angry* and is what most of us feel when it is time to eat and we can't. Science actually supports this idea, which has to do with dropping blood glucose.

Parents, be prepared for the unexpected, and keep snacks in your car and your purse. This could save you a few embarrassing moments of your child losing it. Again, lenience is golden if your child is missing one of the basics.

Lots of research suggests that diet may also affect behavior. If you notice patterns of misbehavior after your child eats certain foods, keep a record. You may need to consult with your pediatrician. It is wise to seek help from those with experience and expertise.

Last, but not least, of what I call the basics is love. If a child isn't feeling loved, you will see it in her behavior. Every child has different needs, but being aware of when your child needs a little extra reassurance is crucial in supporting a healthy, happy child.

As a childcare director, I often had more than 100 children for whom I was responsible within my programs. Our school programs offered children a place where they could relax, play, and learn. Being aware of the basics was essential to providing a place of peace for all of the children.

I often noticed when a child was feeling overwhelmed and needed a bit of extra one-on-one or quiet time. I noted the first sign of this frequently during their interactions with other children. If a child had withdrawn from playing with others or if his play was more confrontational than normal, I knew that something was going on. Noticing before it became a problem was fundamental to maintaining harmony in a group of 75 to 90 children.

This same awareness is just as important in providing a peaceful haven for your family. It is a good idea to schedule

Good parenting does not mean giving him a perfect life.
It means teaching him how to lead a good and happy life
in our imperfect world.
— Author Unknown

one-on-one time with your child as a way to avoid *I need attention* meltdowns. Consider scheduling 45 minutes to an hour to de-stress and unwind from the day. This could be before bedtime. If you have more than one child you may need to decrease the time spent with each one. Try 10 to 15 minutes for each child instead.

Shut down and turn off things that make noise or have a screen. Ending the day with family sharing time and a bedtime story builds connection and strengthens emotional security.

Once the basics are taken care of and clear rules have been established and understood, then we can deliberate discipline. What does discipline look like, and why is it needed? Merriam-Webster defines discipline as: *control gained by enforcing obedience or order.*

We have the responsibility to teach children to make good choices. If we do our job, we should have the expectation that our children will do their job. Setting rules and expectations is essential. Children have the right to receive clear and concise messages. Children should not have to guess what may upset us as the leaders of our families.

Written rules are nice, as this takes the guess-work out of knowing what is expected. It also makes it easy to refer to later when a rule is in question. God gave us a short list of rules in which everything is centered on love.

A new command I give you: Love one another. As I have loved you, so you must love one another. By this everyone will know that you are my disciples, if you love one another."

John 13:34-35 (NIV)

Once children understand what you expect, it is up to them to make the right choice. There should also be consequences for not obeying the rules or meeting expectations. I believe in corporal punishment or spanking. I am confident in my understanding of the Bible regarding this type of discipline. Being secure in what you believe and why permits you to be guilt-free if you choose to spank your child.

Before a parent chooses to spank her child, she should make sure to thoughtfully analyze the pros and cons. What are you hoping to accomplish by using a spanking? Understanding the purpose and goal of a spanking helps you to make a wise decision about when to use this type of discipline. Not every act of disobedience should result in a spanking. Each situation should be evaluated and handled on its own merit.

Whoever spares the rod hates his son, but he who loves him is diligent to discipline him.

Proverbs 13:24 (ESV)

> *Folly is bound up in the heart of a child,*
> *but the rod of discipline drives it far from him.*
>
> Proverbs 22:15 (ESV)

> *Do not withhold discipline from a child;*
> *if you strike him with a rod, he will not die. If you strike him with*
> *the rod, you will save his soul from Sheol.*
>
> Proverbs 23:13-14 (ESV)

> *The rod and reproof give wisdom,*
> *but a child left to himself brings shame to his mother.*
>
> Proverbs 29:15 (ESV)

I used a firm tap to the back of Kenneth's hand when he was one year old and he had touched something that I didn't want him to touch. Later, I spanked Kenneth for different infractions. Again, I don't believe that every mistake should have the same consequences.

I need to share with you a few things about Kenneth to allow you to understand my choices for correcting his behavior long-term. When Kenneth was young, pastors and prophets spoke of a strong anointing on his life. I took him to church with me, and he could sit there for hours, even as a two-year-old. He engaged completely at his young age. He watched, listened, clapped his hands, and praised. It was remarkable.

But this little guy who loved God also had a temper. Sometimes when he didn't want to do something he dug in his heels and refused to obey. When Kenneth was two years old, playing outside with me at his side, he attempted to go into the street. We lived on a quiet cul-de-sac, and I was teaching Kenneth to stay on the grass close to the house. We were playing ball, and if he kicked the ball too hard, the ball rolled into a restricted grassy area.

Kenneth was instructed not to fetch the ball himself but rather to call me instead if the ball rolled too far. Things were going well until he was having so much fun that I think he forgot. He ran into the prohibited area and picked up his ball. I took the ball and swatted his small hand. I told him that he could not go into a certain grassy area, that the cars may not see him and could hurt him. I didn't want him playing outside with me or someone else and forget the boundaries that kept him safe.

He cried for a moment, and we continued to play. He kicked the ball again to the restricted area. He started running to retrieve it but stopped in his tracks, looked back at me, and directed me to get the ball. I gave him kudos and picked up the ball, and we continued our game. We played with balls and other toys for a few days, and it was obvious that Kenneth understood and had the rule down well.

Two weeks later Kenneth and I were playing outside. Kenneth decided that he wanted to get something from the restricted area and crossed out of bounds. I spanked his hand and led him into the house. He was upset, and he intentionally knocked a lamp off of a table. This is the temper to which I referred.

I didn't let his actions distract me from the first issue. I addressed both issues, one at a time, to make sure that he understood them both. I spanked his hand. After he finished crying I marched him outside, and we walked the area in which he could play freely. I shared with him that he might get hurt on the other side and, if that happened, both he and mommy would be sad. He repeated my concern and agreed.

I trotted him back to the lamp and told him that breaking things was not the answer. Kenneth never forgot the rule while playing outside.

I will admit that Kenneth's understanding was quite advanced for a two-year-old. Just for the record, he could not, however, play in the front yard by himself. This life lesson taught him at an early age about boundaries and expectations and that breaking rules had consequences. Kenneth rarely got a spanking at that age.

Sometimes adjusting your child's behavior to a point of acceptability may be an issue. Many books cover this topic. Parents who labor with questions about discipline should seek help. Is corporal punishment okay? If the behavior doesn't improve, should I use time-outs? For what length of time should I suspend privileges for misbehaving?

These questions are personal for every parent in how they choose to raise a child to greatness. Discipline is important, and it takes Godly wisdom to decide what is best. God's word led me to believe that *sparing the rod might not be the best option for raising a child to reach his full potential.*

On the lips of him who has understanding, wisdom is found,
but a rod is for the back of him who lacks sense.
Proverbs 10:13 (ESV)

Do not withhold discipline from a child;
if you strike him with a rod, he will not die.
Proverbs 23:13 (ESV)

Under no circumstances should children ever be beaten or abused. I think it is crucial that children never be spanked by an angry parent. I will confess, however, that I personally didn't always follow this rule, and I regret this tremendously. I made horrible mistakes.

I recall leaving marks on Kenneth when he was in middle school. I thought that he had intentionally been disobedient by not doing his homework. I did spank him with a belt, and the red marks on his thighs and buttocks disappeared after a few hours, but this wasn't acceptable. That was the last time that I ever spanked him.

I didn't spank Kenneth after that because I felt that he was too old to be spanked for it to be effective. It was a short-term pain to try to produce a long-term result.

Kenneth's grades dropped drastically in his first year of middle school. He was 11 turning 12 and just hitting puberty. Looking back later, I realized that if he could have done better, he would have. I viewed his poor grades as my personal failure. I was upset and insistent that he couldn't bring home grades lower than what I thought represented his ability. His poor grades were not a reflection on me or his intellectual abilities.

I now believe that this was a lack of maturity on my part. I made huge blunders in judgment in choosing to spank him for poor grades. Kenneth was bright and had the ability and desire to do what was expected. His mind raced fervently to gain knowledge but not for the purpose of randomly spitting out facts for tests, although he was excellent at that.

He learned to be able to use the information to obtain more information and to find his own answers. He found answers to whatever he was interested in learning. He thirsted for knowledge and understanding.

Kenneth's learning wasn't about making sure that he turned in his homework on time or that it was organized and neat. He wanted to earn good grades, but he wanted knowledge even more than that.

I wish that I had had the wisdom to recognize his gift sooner. I tried bribing, spanking, and threatening my poor son on a weekly basis, hoping that he would earn better grades. It was only by God's grace that his poor little spirit wasn't crushed.

I took Kenneth's unsatisfactory grades as a personal failure. I forgot to focus on his needs. I didn't want a child who got Ds and Fs.

I finally concluded that Kenneth was doing the best he could and that I simply needed to be there to offer support. When I relaxed, his grades improved.

I celebrated that God was in control. I matured and stopped judging Kenneth's grades as if they were mine. I then supported Kenneth in different ways. I focused on making sure that his basic needs were met and encouraged him in positive ways to stay on track.

I purchased an agenda calendar that he felt would help him manage his homework and chores. I followed his lead to make adjustments so that he could improve his grades. I increased our one-on-one time. I showed up at his school and took him to lunch. I even brought his entire chemistry class pizza for lunch one day.

It was all about relationships, personal responsibility, and allowing him to grow. By the time he got to high school, Kenneth's grades really improved, and it was rare that we saw anything below a B.

RECAP

- Make sure that your child's basic needs are met before imposing strict discipline.
- Feed your child healthy food, and monitor food reactions, if necessary.
- Give each child one-on-one time to remind him how special he is.
- Seek help when needed.

CHAPTER NINE

Speak Life

We all fail and have moments when we wish we would have thought things through a little better and made a different choice. We can't go back in time, so having tools that make those failures fewer is a win for everyone. Learning to hold our tongue and speak life to our children is huge. We can never take back words that we have discharged into the world.

I often use the word *power* to express the sheer magnitude of something beyond great, the power of play or the power of love. I stumbled when it came to the power of words. I don't like that phrase. I couldn't find words to express the capacity of our words.

I associate power with positive things, so naturally I am cautious about using it to describe the influence of words. Our words may be spoken for evil and destruction as well as for edification and life. What our words do is up to us and our choices. We can speak life or death. That kind of power is so colossal that it may be both miraculous and catastrophic. This is a dangerous power to hold and not recognize the strength that it possesses regarding our past, our present, and our future.

Understanding that our words are miracles or curses is essential in life. Do you want to release a curse over your life, your child's life, or your marriage? Of course not! Learning to use words as seeds of faith that will bloom blessings into your life is to understand the power of your words. Speak life over your children. Let every word uttered, whether in play or in discipline, be spoken to build your child up.

One of my favorite pastors presented me with an awesome way to choose my words with purpose. Pastor Morrison's advice was to bring to mind the three Ps before opening your mouth: Pause, Pray, and Ponder. When we are distressed and are about to articulate our emotions, it is helpful to recall the three Ps.

Pausing allows the first words that comes to your mind to stay there. Most of the time our first thought isn't always our best.

Prayer helps us gain a Godly perspective and permits our word choice to be seasoned with wisdom.

Let your speech be always with grace, seasoned with salt, that you may know how you ought to answer every man.

Colossians 4:6 (ESV)

To **Ponder** means *to think*.

You all may be familiar with the **THINK** acronym that reminds us to think before we speak. If not, here it is. This is an excellent way to communicate. Examine each thought and the combination of words that you will use to convey that thought. And before releasing the thought through a series of words, question yourself as to whether it is:

True—Is it true?

Helpful—Is it helpful?

Inspiring—Is it inspiring?

Necessary—Is it necessary?

Kind—Is it kind?

Using **THINK** is a helpful way to filter our thoughts before we verbalize them.

Utilizing the **THINK** acronym or the three Ps are beneficial ways to take control of our words during challenging or unexpected times.

When I mention unexpected, I am talking about the morning when you are rushing off to run all of the errands. It has already been one mishap after another, and you are running late. You are fastening your six-year-old into her car seat and realize that she forgot to brush her teeth. She is right in your face, and her breath isn't as fresh as you would like.

You snipe at her, "Yuck, your breath stinks!"

Unfortunately, I once witnessed this horrible interaction between a mother and a child. It was like a kick in my stomach, and the mother's comment wasn't even directed at me.

The young girl cried. "What can I do, Mommy? I'm sorry that I forgot."

It was evident that this little one's day started with an emotional slap. I questioned how this made the child feel. What was the benefit of the mother's disagreeable remark? If there wasn't enough time to run into the house to brush her daughter's teeth, why attack her?

The mother's words were neither kind nor helpful. This is a lesson for all of us. We should all avoid letting stressful moments cause us to use our words as weapons.

On the other hand, what about crafting our words intentionally to uplift and encourage? Parenting with intention demands that we do just that.

We should write letters and notes of encouragement to our children as soon as they can read. Include scriptures in these notes and letters because the word of God is their sword. The word of God is their weapon to combat negative situations that they encounter throughout the day.

Speaking a prayer and words of encouragement daily shields kids from cruel behavior that is devised to tear down their worth and weaken their faith. Let your child hear the word of God each day. It will strengthen his belief that God is capable of all things. You can even read a scripture to babies, and they will reap the benefits. Keep in mind, faith comes by hearing.

Death and life are in the power of the tongue,
and those who love it will eat its fruits.

Proverbs 18:21 (ESV)

"Whoever desires to love life and see good days, let him keep his tongue from evil and his lips from speaking deceit.

1 Peter 3:10 (ESV)

Let no corrupting talk come out of your mouths, but only such as is good for building up, as fits the occasion, that it may give grace to those who hear.

Ephesians 4:29 (ESV)

I tell you, on the Day of Judgment people will give account for every careless word they speak, for by your words you will be justified, and by your words you will be condemned."

Matthew 12:36-37 (ESV)

*Set a guard, O Lord, over my mouth;
keep watch over the door of my lips!*

Psalms 141:3 (ESV)

*But no human being can tame the tongue.
It is a restless evil, full of deadly poison.*

James 3:8 (NIV)

If anyone thinks he is religious and does not bridle his tongue but deceives his heart, this person's religion is worthless.

James 1:26 (ESV)

*Out of my distress I called on the Lord;
the Lord answered me answered me and set me free.*

Psalms 118:5 (ESV)

There is one whose rash words are like sword thrusts,
but the tongue of the wise brings healing.

Proverbs 12:18 (ESV)

When words are many, transgression is not lacking,
but whoever restrains his lips is prudent.

Proverbs 10:19 (ESV)

And the tongue is a fire, a world of unrighteousness. The tongue
is set among our members, staining the whole body, setting on fire
the entire course of life, and set on fire by hell.

James 3:6 (ESV)

The heart of the righteous ponders how to answer, but the mouth
of the wicked pours out evil things.

Proverbs 15:28 (ESV)

A gentle tongue is a tree of life, but perverseness in it breaks the spirit.

Proverbs 15:4 (ESV)

Know this, my beloved brothers: let every person be quick to hear, slow to speak, slow to anger;

James 1:19 (ESV)

*Whoever guards his mouth preserves his life;
he who opens wide his lips comes to ruin.*

Proverbs 13:3 (ESV)

So then faith comes by hearing, and hearing by the word of God.

Romans 10:17 (ESV)

Uttering words in faith and witnessing God move is something that still thrusts me into immediate awe of God. Have you ever needed the weather to change and then spoke to it, and it responded? I have. It is times like that that build faith for more substantial trials. Each victory is God showing us His faithfulness. Every time we pray with confidence and God moves on our behalf, it is a testimony for us to look back on and draw strength for the present.

Speaking in faith is powerful. I often reminisce about a day when words spoken took my faith to a new maturity.

Speak Life

I drove my daughter, Nicole, to high school each morning because she wasn't interested in taking on the responsibility of driving. Those are her words, not mine. In fact, she didn't drive until she was 19. I actually cherished this time with her, it was blessing. I realize it even more so now that she is grown. I had her captured in my car for 45 minutes on the way to school and 45 minutes to an hour on the way home.

Many times she wanted me to stop for a snack, so the ride home was a little longer depending on where we went. In the mornings she rarely mumbled more than five sentences, so I talked. I told her how precious and smart she was. I shared words of encouragement and scriptures. Some mornings we listened to the radio to another one of my favorite pastors, Pastor Bob. Other mornings we listened to praise music, but every morning we prayed before she went into school. I pretty much ruled the mornings.

The afternoons were completely different. Nicole was reserved at school, but she enjoyed talking. By the time I picked her up after school she was an explosion of words and animation. She shared about her entire day, from morning drop-off to afternoon pick-up. She was descriptive and detailed in her accounts. It was like I saw a picture and read a biography of her teachers' lives before I even met them. I could pick them out of a lineup and get it right every time without ever having seen them once.

One morning we were late to school. I can't recall why we were late, but late was a mammoth fiasco for Nicole. Nicole had a 4.8 grade point average and was ranked number one out of 631 students in her class. She didn't like to be late or miss a day of school. She was in the tenth grade at the time.

It is important to note this because this changed big-time when she was a senior, but that is another story. I should disclose that her attitude about missing school and being late changed, not her grades.

So we were late, and Nicole was almost in tears. This was heartbreaking because this girl rarely ever cried. I tried to encourage her and tell her that things would work out, but she wasn't having it.

Her hands shook, and I could feel her anxiety. She seemed exasperated by each word I spoke.

She interrupted me, and in a short, abrupt, and distressed tone scoffed, "Can God stop time?"

I remember feeling somewhat fearful, as if she had just challenged God.

"God can do all things," I replied.

I spoke in faith. Neither Nicole nor I said another word for the remainder of the ride to school. When we arrived there, students, parents, and teachers stood in the parking lot. We locked eyes and then gawked at the clock in disbelief. She was definitely five minutes late.

Her face, once contorted from stress, was now overtaken by bewilderment. We stared at each other, puzzled by all the action in the parking lot, but we didn't utter a word. She hopped out of the car and jogged into the school.

I whispered a prayer for my daughter and drove to work. I thought about the morning drama all day.

When I picked Nicole up from school that afternoon she bounced into the car and began her usual narration of the entire day as if the morning catastrophe had never happened.

I interrupted her this time. "Nicole, did you get in trouble for being late?"

"No. The clocks stopped working this morning, so the bells didn't ring, and the teachers couldn't mark any students late."

"So, it was like God stopped time for you this morning?"

She smiled and agreed. Again, words spoken in faith may change the outcome of what you think should happen by all reasonable standards.

Do you recall the story about when Jesus was hungry and stood in front of a tree that bore no fruit? Jesus cursed the tree, and it died. He also spoke to a dead man, and he came back from the dead.

Our words can give life or even stop time. We must use our words carefully and watch the faithfulness of God shine. God can do anything, even stop time!

RECAP

- Use the three Ps—**Pause, Pray, Ponder.**
- Craft your words wisely—THINK.
- Customize your words to encourage your child.

CHAPTER TEN

How Long is the Season?

For everything there is a season,
a time for every activity under heaven.

Ecclesiastes 3:1 (NLT)

Parenting infants is exhausting, and you will miss lots of sleep. But keep in mind that this is just one season. The seasons of parenting each stage of our children's lives will go by quicker than you can imagine. There will inevitably be times in the midst of a season that that season seems to last forever. But rest assured, every season ends. The stages of parenting change, but you will be a parent forever.

I like to share that a good parent's words of wisdom and insightful knowledge will live on from generation to generation. What do you want your legacy to be?

> *Legacy—A story that is yet to be written*
> *for which you hold the pen.*
>
> — Juliet Funt, CEO, WhiteSpace at Work

I believe that wise parents will leave as their legacy words of wisdom, love, and a testament to the goodness of a living God. Crafting a legacy that impacts the kingdom of God for His glory calls for us to gaze past the temporal and focus on the eternal. Create heirlooms that will continue to grow and bless each generation as treasured gifts that will last forever.

> *We will not hide them from their children,*
> *but tell to the coming generation the glorious deeds of the* LORD,
> *and His might, and the wonders that He has done.*
>
> Psalms 78:4 (ESV)

My grandmother often preached, "*Nothing beats a failure except a try. God don't like ugly, and life is too short to carry around baggage that you don't need.*" She was full of wise adages. One of her favorites was, "*Keep your room clean, you never know who might see it.*"

The wealth of her words of wisdom are forever imprinted in my mind, even though she left this world many years ago. I still hear her words in my mind. The funny thing is that they're her words, but I hear my mom's voice echoing them. Why? Grandmother may have passed on, but she left her words with my mom, who passed them on to me. I then passed them on to my children. They have been passed from generation to generation.

A good man leaves an inheritance to his children's children,
but the sinner's wealth is laid up for the righteous.

Proverbs 13:22 (NIV)

You shall love the LORD your God with all your heart
and with all your soul and with all your might.
And these words that I command you today shall be
on your heart. You shall teach them diligently to your children,
and shall talk of them when you sit in your house,
and when you walk by the way, and when you lie down,
and when you rise.

Deuteronomy 6:5-7 (ESV)

But the steadfast love of the LORD is from everlasting to
everlasting on those who fear Him,
and His righteousness to children's children.

Psalms 103:17 (ESV)

> *Therefore, I intend always to remind you of these qualities, though you know them and are established in the truth that you have. I think it right, as long as I am in this body, to stir you up by way of reminder, since I know that the putting off of my body will be soon, as our Lord Jesus Christ made clear to me. And I will make every effort so that after my departure you may be able at any time to recall these things.*
>
> 1 Peter 1:12-15 (ESV)

I heard a pastor preach that parenting has three stages. Teacher is the first stage, coach is the next stage, and cheerleader is the last stage. The first stage, as the teacher, is hands-on and directive.

During the middle stage, as a coach, you allow your child to play the game, you provide her with training and the knowledge about the rules of the game. The coach stands on the sidelines and only advises during time-outs, halftime, or if a player is pulled out of the game due to injury or misconduct.

And in the final stage, as a cheerleader, parents celebrate each time their child scores and takes a knee when he gets hurt. Our children will take some hard blows in the game, so a cheerleader taking a knee represents supporting them and reminding them of their victories.

Some might perceive this as an over-simplification, but I like it.

Someone once told me that parenting is over when your children are grown and successfully living on their own. I hope that no parent would accept this view, but especially one who has committed to parenting with intent. Why?

As parents our lives should be about continuously role-modeling, since we will ultimately encounter challenges as we age. How we cope and find solutions is a roadmap from which our children may learn.

Our healthy lifestyle may demonstrate love. Actively pursuing healthy life choices allows us to take some burdens off of our children and establish a possible strategy for them in their later years.

Parenting doesn't stop. As parents we are called to go before our children to show them how to live life through every stage. We will grow old by God's grace with our children seeing how we handle the process. Our life should reflect our Savior all the way to the end.

Let parents bequeath to their children not riches,
but the spirit of reverence.

— Plato

Embrace the season that you are in, and as kids advise, stay in your lane. Staying in your lane means doing only what is on your path. As a grandparent, it is not our job to raise our grandchildren. We are the cheerleaders! We cheer our adult children on and unconditionally love them and our grandbabies. We are here to remind them of God's promises and to point to His victories in our family.

Yes, we help when petitioned to do so. Yes, if you are led to give advice or warnings, do so sparingly and only after prayerful deliberation.

I sometimes think of the seasons of parenting like the seasons of the year. Spring reminds me of new buds forming, green leaves sprouting, and short, refreshing rain showers.

Early in parenting, things were fresh, new, and exciting. I anticipated what was going to sprout up or happen next. It was spring. My children were young buds zealously soaking up what the world had to offer.

Summer parenting ushered in long, hot days of repetition. Wake up, go to school, eat dinner, go to sleep, and repeat. Our family had to find ways to replenish the excitement of life. We sprinkled in play, vacations, and family fun times.

During autumn things started to fall away. Our children went off to college, and our responsibilities as parents became less hands-on. It was a time of reflection. Thoughts of my expectations for my children's lives fell away. It was time to let them live their own lives. Autumn is beautiful as the leaves change colors. In autumn we saw that our children were changing from child to adult, and this was lovely.

The winter of parenting shows in my white hair and the wisdom that living has provided. It is cozy, restful, and filled with moments of quiet stillness. It offers times to be insightful and delight in the past. Our children are our friends if we did a few things right.

> *Grandchildren are the crown of the aged,*
> *and the glory of children is their fathers.*
> Proverbs 17:6 (ESV)

This is not a chapter about schedules, consistency, or discipline. It's about finding pleasure in the moments of life and remembering to **PLAY,** relax, and relish being a parent or grandparent. This chapter is not meant to erase what has been shared above but rather is a reminder that we are human beings and that life needs spontaneous moments of happiness!

I love that God reminds us to rest. Our rest is so important to God that He put it in the Ten Commandments as a mandate. He understands us in such detail that He instructs us to rest on the Sabbath day. He identified that we would be so engrossed in our lives that we would forget to rest if we didn't make it a priority. This is for parents in every season but especially in later seasons.

I have one last acronym to remind you to enjoy the lane that you are in. The acronym is INSPIRE. This one is to help you to not forget to relax and adore your children and grandchildren.

Invest. Use your time, money, and effort to build up your children, grandchildren, and family! Take time to write thoughtful notes and set play dates. Strong, quality relationships are instrumental to living a life of abundance.

> **N**ourish family with supportive actions. Find out where you are needed and be there.
>
> **S**hine What is your story or gift? Share it with the world.
>
> **P**osition yourself as the peace-maker.
>
> **I**nfluence those around you with your vulnerability, empathy, and integrity.
>
> **R**eflect on the good times and God's faithfulness. Take a moment to reminisce about happy times; laugh and share. Pull out pictures or videos to add visuals to the memories.
>
> **E**mbrace every moment as if it was your last. If you only had an hour to live, what would be the most important thing to accomplish? Would it be a spotless house or how much

money you make? Take time to highlight what is important, and sometimes that means counting your blessings. People, not material things, are our true treasures. Put worry aside, and focus on what you do have. Enjoy the moments of relaxing without guilt. Just be.

So don't worry about tomorrow, for tomorrow will bring its own worries. Today's trouble is enough for today.

Matthew 6:34 (NLT)

Yes, parenting is hard, and it is a lot of work. But we must include times when we shout out loud that spur-of-the-moment fun is happening now!

Academics, discipline, and structure are things that we should desire. But more importantly, cultivating an intimate, loving relationship with God is at the top of the list. Then we may work on our relationships with others.

*Jesus replied: "Love the L*ORD *your God with all your heart and with all your soul and with all your mind." This is the first and greatest commandment. And the second is like it: "Love your neighbor as yourself." All the Law and the Prophets hang on these two commandments.*

Matthew 22:37-40 (NIV)

It is hard to schedule rest, but this is a must. We not only need to schedule rest, we need to listen to our hearts and bodies and adjust when we need more rest. We function best when we take time to rest. Sometimes we need rest in different areas of our lives. Our body could need rest but so could our mind and spirit.

Life may sometimes be overwhelming and seem to demand too much from us. But God cautions that we shouldn't worry or have anxiety over situations that we cannot control. If we find ourselves worried and stressed, it means that we need some spiritual rest. Find your peace and refresh your soul by spending time with God, praising, listening to music, or meditating. It is okay to take a time-out. In fact, it is necessary. If possible, schedule yourself a get-away and make it happen.

Peace I leave with you; my peace I give you.
I do not give to you as the world gives.
Do not let your hearts be troubled and do not be afraid.
John 14:27 (NIV)

Thank you for letting me share with you. This has been a long journey, one on which I learned new things along the way. While writing this book, one question seemed to plaque me. *Do all parents care about what I cared about as a parent?*

Over my many years of working with parents in various schools, I have noticed that moms are quite sensitive when it comes to others questioning their style of parenting. Often we contemplate with anguish whether we are making the right choices while at the same time not wanting others to see our vulnerability.

My niece once was conducting research about women's issues and told me that women feel most vulnerable when questioned about their parenting skills more than any other area of their lives. As mothers, we would like to think that we were born with the ability to be a good mom.

The aforementioned African proverb is key to every parent's success. *It takes a village to raise a child.* You cannot do it by yourself. I realize that we covered this earlier, but this idea needs to be received without reservation. You must reach out to others and permit them to bless you and your children. What is cool is that they, too, will be blessed when you allow them to help you.

When God uses people for His glory, all reap the rewards of a fuller life. Find a teacher, church members, a person with a proven track record on raising children, or join a parenting group.

RECAP

- Be the inspiration. INSPIRE.

  Invest

  Nourish

  Shine

  Position yourself as the peacekeeper

  Influence

  Reflect

  Embrace

- Highlight what is important.

CHAPTER ELEVEN

107 Perspectives

In closing, I decided to take my own advice. It wasn't my idea. This concept came from a quiet voice on my drive home one day. I was pondering the fact that I had finished the book, and yet I heard God whisper, *Not yet. I want you to reach out to other parents to finish this book.* I must admit that the village didn't let me down. I learned a lot, laughed a lot, and appreciated the honesty that so many others were willing to share.

This last chapter may have been the hardest part of writing this book. It pushed me once more to expand my horizons and disregard the fear. It forced me to forget my comfort zone. I normally don't like to talk to people I don't know. I am an introvert, and asking people to help me with this book was particularly challenging. I approached people at the airport, the laundry mat, and the grocery store. I spent time in malls from New York City to Salt Lake City, asking folks a few questions in our brief encounter. Sometimes they shared where they lived and how many children they had. Many stayed on script and didn't share details.

As I eased up to people, I often sensed their uneasiness about an advancing stranger. I could perceive their body language as they expected the worst. I often wondered if they thought that I was about to beg for money or sell them the latest in new gadgets.

However, I simply opened a dialogue. "Excuse me, I'm sorry to bother you, but may I ask you a few quick questions. I'm writing a book. Are you a parent?"

If someone responded yes, I posed my question. "What is your favorite part about parenting?"

With that question, relief spread across faces, bodies loosened up, and in most cases, immediate happiness followed. More times than not a wide smile grew, and eyes glowed as they imagined their favorite moments of parenting. I encountered so many proud parents!

I hope you delight in this last chapter. My desire is that this chapter will be encouragement for your soul on days when you feel a bit overwhelmed or on days when you just need some sunshine. It's a reflection on the best parts of parenting, from the perspective of many others. I hope that this chapter helps you keep in mind why you are doing what you are doing.

I have shared with you here 107 of the responses that I got to my question.

1. Madeline, Puerto Rico, age 66, three adult children.
   Parenting is love. It is an honor. The best part is God's love flowing through me into my children and the love that they give back.

2. Ethel, Louisiana, age 75, three adult children.
   My favorite part of parenting was when kids are little and don't question you. They just do and believe what you tell them.

3. Duvonn, New Mexico, age 58, two adult boys.
   Seeing them grow up to become productive adults.

   Duvonn then asked me a question. *Can I tell you what I would like to be able to answer? I wish I could say seeing them grow up to love the Lord like I do. But all things are possible with God. They are still alive, so it can happen.*

4. Ashley, age 30, three-year-old girl and eight-year-old boy.
   The delight in parenting is even through all of the tough times with my daughter and my son, seeing a smile on their faces and knowing that my husband and I produced that happiness. Their contentment makes everything worth it.

5. Yolanda, age 48, five children, ages 18, 16, 14, 12, and 4.

> *Watching your kids grow up and seeing what they become. Realizing that they will live a full life once they are grown and embracing that I had played a part in it.*

6. Quanita, Denver, age 50, two adult children, one female, one male.

    Parenting pleasures are that there are so many stages, from when a child is born to when he is an adult. You see where they start as they grow into their own person. My daughter had a rough time, but watching her mature and calm down and do well is rewarding. She made a nice transformation. I am thankful that God gave me a chance to be a parent. Not everyone is meant to be a parent or gets the chance to become one.

7. Tim, age 55, two adult children.

    I think the highlight of parenting is when your children get to the age to make difficult decisions, and their choices make them better. As a parent all you have to do and all you can do and should do is stand back and let them make those choices for themselves. You know they've made the right decisions for themselves when those decisions turn out positive in their lives and they are well-adjusted citizens. You know you've done a good job as a parent.

8. Natalie, age 42, one-year-old daughter.

   The unconditional love that flows both ways.

9. Danica, age 28, three-year-old.

   I love the snuggles and rejoicing that you contributed more to the world than just yourself. And through your child you have a vast reach.

10. Emily, age 38, five children, ages 1 through 12.

    My husband is a patent attorney, and this is something that we talk about often. We have a saying in our family that we call a family paycheck. And it's when you get to see your child come to an understanding of a principle or concept that you have been teaching her. When she uses this learned skill it is like receiving a paycheck. Seeing things click for your child is a payday for you as a parent.

11. Amy, age 42, three children, ages 5, 9, and 12.

    It is seeing their faces light up and receiving their hugs.

12. Dick, age 88, two boys.

    Well, my wife is the best part of parenting. My generation worked a lot of long days. My wife did a commendable job, and our kids turned out compassionate, charitable, and noble because of her. And she learned to make the most fabulous meatloaf in the world.

13. Sumiko, Philippines, age 85.

    My English is poor, but kids grow up and are good. No trouble. I like when they come home and eat and visit together.

14. Rita, age 68, two children, ages 38 and 34.

    My favorite thing about parenting is watching your children grow up and become their own person. I almost retorted, "grandchildren." They are truly wonderful!

15. Bassant, age 39.

    When I see that all of my hard work is being rewarded because my son is learning...and when he shrieks, "I love you."

16. Linda, age 65, five children, 22 grandchildren.

    Grandkids and when kids grow up and leave home.

    Okay, can I answer again? It's hard being a parent, but I have kids that warm my heart. The second-to-none experience of being a parent is when they love each other, and the family unity.

    The unbeatable delight of parenting is the growth of who they are and how they teach and stretch you. Parenting challenges you, and you learn so much from your kids. Parenting is true love. It puts the joy in your posterity! You see the love of each moment after they are gone. But they are always teaching you, and you are always teaching even when they are grown and live somewhere else.

17. Denise, age 55, son age 25 and daughter age 21.

    Parenting well is the prospect of seeing your kids as they mature and become well-adjusted adults. Oh, another thing is seeing their faith journey. That is so rewarding, watching them mature in their faith. They are truly beautiful people.

18. Gary, age 71.

    Parenting ecstasy is seeing kids develop into their own people. This is evidence that you did something right!

19. Fred, age 54.

    I don't have an answer. I wasn't a parent. I was incarcerated when my kids were babies. I wasn't a part of raising them. But I think that it would be knowing that you have a child to carry on your legacy and when you are old someone to take care of you.

20. Natalie, age 48, three children.

    Watching my children grow up and develop a relationship with the Lord and care for others.

21. Marissa, age 27, one son, age 7.

    The best thing and the worst thing about parenting is watching kids grow up. It is a huge responsibility being cognizant that I help foster my son's growth. It's my job to make sure that he is thoughtful, caring, honest, and cares for others. The worst thing is that as he grows he moves closer to leaving me, and we have different personalities, and sometimes we don't see eye to eye on matters.

22. John, age 52, two boys, ages 10 and 14.

    I want to see what they will be when they grow up. It is exciting to be aware that you are playing a part in the future.

23. Rosa, Korea, age 39, four children, ages 5, 7, 10, and 12.

    English is my second language, I may need help translating words.

    What make me cherish parenting is that my children think that I am the most beautiful woman in the world. I am hard on my kids. I feel like I struggle often in parenting. They love me, and I can gaze into their eyes and know this.

    I need to be the person who helps them be prepared for life. The culture is different here, and I want to help them navigate through life so that they can do it by themselves proficiently. I want them to excel academically to make life easier for them.

24. Joanna, age 30, two-year-old.

    My special sentiment about parenting is the love that your child has for you. Kids are so forgiving of everything that you have done wrong. They have a heart for you.

25. Morgan, age 24, one child, one year old.

    The treasure of parenting is the outcome. Watching them grow and being proud that you did it right!

26. Hia, age 25, one daughter, two months old.

    My favorite part of parenting is watching my daughter grow. Each day she changes. She is my daily motivation to be better and to do better.

27. Nichelle, age 25, one daughter, six months old.

    The crown of parenting is the drive that you acquire for your child, which carries into all areas of your life. The opportunity to make someone else happy is another joyous incentive of parenting. It is incredible when you realize how many people care about you and your baby. You get so much help.

28. Stephone, age 33, one son, age seven.

    The most wondrous part of parenting is the ah ha moment. When you see your kid comprehend an idea and life starts to make sense to them. I am excited for the moments when I teach my son a concept and he uses it in his life because he understands what I taught him.

As a parent you are always throwing random stuff up against the wall and hoping that information sticks. I know that I am doing something right when I see my son applying the knowledge that I taught him correctly to a situation.

29. Gabrielle, age 21, one child, one year old.

    A parenting high is seeing your child grow and learn new things, like dancing and making friends. Also, helping him become better at doing stuff.

30. Rano, Middle East, age 44.

    Grandchildren! I have more time with my grandchildren. I was busy working all the time with my kids. I love that I now get to spend time playing with my grandbaby.

31. Hardy, age 73, two children.

    The most gratifying part of parenting is that you have the opportunity to have your finger on the pulse of the world. Even if kids have to go the long way around but they still come out successful, you know that you did something right.

32. Amy, age 34, three boys.

Note from the author: Amy initially refused to talk to me. I sat in my car trying to build up the nerve to ask people I didn't know my question about parenting.

Each time I went out was so difficult, and instead of getting easier, the more people I questioned the more challenging it felt. As I sat there giving myself a pep talk and talking with God, I saw three boys running around. One was seven-ish, the second was five-ish, and the third was perhaps three years old.

The middle boy fell. He already had a bandage around his left hand and a large beige bandage on his knee. When he fell he screamed as if he had broken his leg, maybe even a couple of other bones. I could hear him quite well with all of my windows rolled up.

Immediately the oldest boy ran back to his fallen comrade. He surrounded the boy with his entire body. With the older boy's arm around the hurt youngster's chest, he gently rocked him back and forth, and the screams quickly faded to a whimper and then stopped. The youngest boy stood over them and watched. In less than three minutes they were all running and happy again.

That's when I eagerly stepped out of my car. I expectantly looked down the path and saw mom, Amy, approaching. I was inspired to hear what her favorite moments of parenting were. I wanted to learn her secrets to parenting so much that I forgot to be afraid to approach her.

I pranced up to her and hurriedly introduced myself. I stated that I was writing a book. I asked her if she had a quick moment to answer a few questions for me. She snapped at me!

Since I had just witnessed such kindness and compassion from one brother to another, from such young children, I wanted her answer, so *no* wasn't an option for me.

I skipped alongside of her to keep up as I shared my battle to just get up the nerve to ask parents a question for this chapter of the book. I confessed to her that after seeing her boys I really hoped she would communicate her thoughts and wisdom to parenting.

She halted, looked me in the eyes, and did indeed divulge the power behind her parenting. And I am glad she did! Thanks, Amy.

I had a friend once attest to me: It is an honor to raise the next generation of men. She actually expressed this to me even before I had children. I always held onto those words and believe them and embrace that honor.

> 33. Mario, age 41, three children.
>
> *The most rewarding aspects of parenting is that you learn so much about your children and yourself. It is hard but rewarding, and you contribute to a life legacy.*

34. Rachel, age 38.

The most enthralling incentive of being a parent is the additional emotion that you tap into that you never felt before. You love so much more in a way that is hard to describe, so much more intensely. You feel more grateful, your admiration is enormous. This is a little person that you would do anything for, and this is what makes parenting worth it.

35. Anita, age 62, 33-year-old son.

This is an unbelievably difficult question. I am lost in thought.

Wait, the sunshine of parenting is grasping that there is someone who is always a part of you. They will belong to you forever. You can get divorced, but your children are always yours. There isn't a better relationship. They bring fullness into your heart forever.

36. Noah, age 67, two sons.

Loving your kids and gaining a close relationship with them is the awesome stuff you get when you are a parent. And can I add grandchildren?

37. Pam, age 63, 37-year-old son.

First, I guess my answer is predicated on the fact of where we lived. I raised my son in Compton, California. So the wonderful part about parenting was raising him to the age *of 38 without him becoming a gang-banger or a drug dealer or a drug user or murdered. I like him. I like his personality. He is a good guy, and he makes me happy.*

38. Katlynn, age 37.

The finest moments of parenting are watching my daughter develop and learn new things. Children make you appreciate life more. We are older parents, and now having the opportunity to raise a daughter is a new challenge that we are thrilled about. It is like nothing else.

39. Lyn, age 48.

The most fulfilling part about parenting for me is when I get home from work, and my daughter looks at me with her big, bright eyes and shouts, 'Daddy!'

40. Jessica, age 32.

The unsurpassed gift of parenting is that children find delight in everything and help you find it too!

41. Dan, age 31.

My favorite slice of parenting is passing down traditions from the past and making new ones.

42. Ben, age 38.

The biggest reward of parenting is seeing kids grow up. It is something new and different every day. The way they act, the way they think, and even their physical abilities are different each day.

43. Kara, age 47.

Prize-winning parenting is to see all of the fine attributes that are an extension of you. All of the admirable attributes that continue in someone else brings such completeness. Kids are people too, and you affect the future through them.

44. Corrie, age 32.

One perk of parenting is seeing your kids happy at the end of the day. When they light up the room with appreciation, love, and fun it is a terrific reward.

45. Krysta, age 32.

The most heartwarming thing about parenting is seeing your kids learn. As accountable parents, we must teach them.

46. Gary, age 65.

Watching your kids grow into who they are, who they will become, their interests, their personality, and their goals and dreams is what makes parenting worth it. I like watching how my kids will impact the world.

47. Tamara, age 51.

The wow of parenting is the unconditional love. No matter what you do as a parent, your kids still love you. Kids are so merciful.

48. Glenda, age 67, two adult children.

Seeing my kids gain understanding when they learn about themselves and the people within their world.

49. Stephanie, age 54, three adult sons.

The fabulous part about parenting is being able to love someone faithfully and forever.

50. Lyne, age 67.

The most satisfying part about parenting is that my daughter has been the center of my world and my closest friend. She is a teacher and brings such delight to my life. I was a single mom, and I think that is why I was so lucky to have her.

51. Samira, age 58.

The greatest return of parenting is that you do everything for others with pleasure. All the sacrificing you do isn't a burden because it is accomplished with love. Giving gives happiness and elation back to you, and that is the ultimate feeling ever.

52. Casey, age 43.

The part of parenting that is the most fulfilling for me is fostering skills and nurturing your kids' natural talents so that they may accomplish their goals. It is my pleasure to help them along the way to reaching their dreams.

53. Michael, age 82.

I would say being able to watch your children do something worthwhile for others.

Children are not a distraction from more important work. They are the most important work.

— CS. Lewis

54. Amanda, age 32, six boys.

The most gratifying experience of parenting is watching kids grow up, laugh, live, and love. It is the sweetness of each day that my kids bring to my life. As a mother raising boys, even though I have my husband, I feel like it's my job to teach them to be gentlemen. I want them to be old-school and hold doors open, say please and thank you, and remember to respect everyone. I want them to be compassionate and kind, and they are. This is a rarity, but it is important.

My boys take pride in people noticing their manners and how respectful they are. It actually brings pure contentment to their faces.

My eldest son saved my life. I was on a bad track. I was doing drugs. I got pregnant after my fourth date with my now husband, but by the grace of God I stopped doing drugs! I have been clean now for fourteen years.

55. Jerry, age 65.

Seeing my children happy and watching them grow into what God called them to be is the unequalled part of parenting.

56. Diane, age 62.

The most worthwhile part of parenting is being a grandparent! Okay, also, this is a tough question. The most marvelous part of parenting is loving your kids fully. Love seems easy, but it is not.

It means putting in the work to help kids to be their best. It means sometimes forgetting about yourself and focusing on them, putting them first. It means staying up late and waking up early, getting no sleep when your kids need you. It is knowing that all of your hard work will be rewarded with their successes in life and their failures if they learn from them.

57. Christy, age 41, two girls.

The most spectacular part of parenting is the sense of accomplishment you achieve from seeing your children's triumph.

58. Angela, age 46.

The most magnificent part of parenting is the ability to give your kids the tools, guidance, and love to be successful. It is astonishing being trusted to develop a little human being. You try to give them everything they need, but you are also aware that sometimes they will face adversity, which is also the fuel that propels children toward success. Children are resilient.

59. Courtney, age 35, three boys.

What makes parenting worth it are those moments when you see the sheer enchantment on your child's face, whether he is giggling over something or is in awe and wonder over something that he has never experienced before. It is in the moments when they question something that expresses the innocence of children. Those are the moments that keep you going because the hard stuff can be so incredibly overwhelming.

When you see the fruit of your labors, after making it through a difficult season and you see that it wasn't in vain, you know that your kid has matured and learned. You cry happy tears. Maybe the best thing is that being a parent makes you a better person.

60. Yolanda, age 51, two boys.

The monumental points in parenting are seeing my kids grapple with an issue, figure it out, and make right decisions.

61. Keith, age 54.

Watching my kids flourish as adults and seeing my hard work and sacrifice pay off is the most extraordinary part of parenting.

62. Tera, age 52.

There are so many features to express about the wonderment of parenting. I'm in a totally new season of parenting. So, I would have to say that I learn something every day from this wise soul who keeps me grounded, humble, and in enormous gratitude and love. I admire her spirit.

63. Terra, age 41.

The unrivaled goodness of parenting is that I have learned so much about myself as a human being, a woman, and a person through being a parent. I get to travel in the life journey of my kiddos. It is awesome.

"It's okay that your parents aren't perfect; no one's are. And it's okay that they didn't have any perfect children either; no one's are. You see, our whole purpose is to strive together in righteousness, overcoming our weaknesses day by day. Don't ever give up on each other."
—Ardeth Kapp

64. Trish, age 55.

As a Christian mama, the most laudable part of parenting is teaching my children about the love and salvation of Jesus Christ.

65. Lance, age 43.

This is a tough question for me right now. My kids are 17 and 15, so I have to examine that question often. Being honest about it, everything would be my answer to the most glorious parts of parenting.

66. Drinda, age 41, two children.

I have one kid at each end of the spectrum, one is gifted, and one is special needs. The bounty of parenting is seeing my kids face a hard challenge and come out on the other side with self-confidence and success. They figure out how to muster up the strength to accept the challenge and win.

It is my job to set them up with skills, confidence, and support and then step back and let them go.

67. Pam, age 55, six adult children.

    Parenting goodies are that you are allowed the opportunity to start out with incredible little people and raise them to be your best friends, and it's a delicious surprise.

"A child can teach an adult three things… To be happy for no reason. To always be busy with something. And to know how to demand with all his might that which he desires."

— Paulo Coelho

68. Chris, age 55.

    I am a teacher, so I think this affects my answer. I think the most wonderful thing about parenting is watching kids learn and discover the world.

69. Jerimiah, age 26.

    My first answer is when the baby poops, and it blows through the diaper and oozes down his entire back.

    Okay, my real answer to the greatest thing about parenting is the responsibility that it gives you. You have a purpose that is bigger than yourself. Even if you are sick you go to work because you have people counting on you.

And I like my first answer too, because it reminds you to laugh at life and be flexible.

70. Cecilia, age 25.

   The most wonderful bonus from parenting is the unconditional love you receive. You are perfect in your child's eyes.

71. Marie, Haiti, age 44.

   The glorious facets of parenting are always placing your kids first and watching the results. As parents we want the best for our kids. I push my kids forward and do whatever I can to help them achieve their goals. They didn't ask to be born. I brought them into this world, and it is my duty to equip them for what is ahead of them. They work hard, I work hard, and we make each other proud.

72. Jinney, age 59.

   The superb part of parenting is seeing my kids grow into respectful, responsible adults. I like seeing the values that I have been teaching them over and over again finally sink in. I would miss the whole point of parenting if I didn't feel the unconditional love that I have given them and that they give back to me.

73. Elaine, age 67.

   There isn't just one magnificent moment or component about parenting, there are many moments and factors.

Some of the greatest things are love, growth, and happiness. It is way too much good stuff to answer with one sentence, paragraph, or even a book. It would take a lifetime.

74. Despiana, age 52.

What is the best part about parenting? It is different for each stage of of a child's life, but I'm going to steal a page from Kris Kardashian's book. Mothers love and worry about their children. The love is the number one part.

> *There is no such thing as a perfect parent so just be a real one.*
> — Sue Atkins

75. Susan, age 69.

My answer is reflective of my experience as an adoptive mom and comes from a deep longing to be a parent. The supreme substance of parenting is pure and utter fulfillment and the pleasure of watering, cultivating, and being a part of watching kids grow into adulthood. This is a reflection of God's heart. And even when it's hard, you discern that the work that you are doing is for the kingdom of God.

76. Kathy, age 72.

The most fulfilling compensation of parenting is the unconditional love of a child. They don't judge or hold faults against you. You can make all kinds of mistakes, and a kid finds a way to forgive you and continue to love you.

77. Juanita, age 40.

The stuff that makes me the most happy being a parent is when I see my child take on something new and exciting, and I experience it through her eyes. Her win becomes a part of me.

78. Jenny, age 55.

The awesome part of parenting is that the love for your children is so big that it has an abiding lure, and it drives you closer to God!

79. Justin, age 39.

Happy parenting is seeing your child come to an understanding about something and learn from his mistakes. It is watching and helping your kid traverse the learning process of life. It is them encountering life and coming out on the other side a better person.

80. Stacey, age 45.

The most gratifying part about parenting is having the opportunity to love deeply and guide someone to the kingdom and love of Christ.

There are no perfect parents, and there are no perfect children, but there are many perfect moments along the way.

—Dave Willis

81. Dana, age 49.

What I love about parenting is the opportunity to mold and influence a young mind. It's the aspect of communicating an abundant love, life, and surrendering your heart. It grants you a life connection that will last forever. Parenting warms my heart and is a blessing.

82. Michelle, age 53.

Parenting requires me to really focus on the guidelines of what God declares about having our lives in order. God is a God of love and order.

The appreciation in parenting starts with a strong marriage between my husband and me. This allows me to embrace my role as a parent. I am designed to be a helpmate and supporter to the leader of our family, my husband. I must respect and appreciate my husband's leadership as he guides the family into a relationship with our heavenly Father.

When a marriage honors God with true love, commitment, and selflessness, parenting is awesome. Our children are always watching and learning from us at every age. This is the joy of parenting.

83. Rebecca, age 38.

The most rewarding part of parenting is watching my children experience traditions in our family for the first time. Observing their eyes light up as they learn something new brings tears of glee to my eyes.

84. Arthur, age 38.

The ultimate thrill obtained from parenting is when the light bulb goes on in my child's head. And then I realize that what I've been preaching hasn't been going in one ear and out the other. That's a million-dollar feeling! Combine that with seeing them happy, and it's unimaginable gladness!

85. Kim, age 42.

The finest part of parenting is the awe-inspiring and grand feeling that I experienced just in becoming a parent. What a humbling task God has given me. He entrusted me to raise two princesses to be wonderful adults.

86. Kim, age 54.

The most majestic thing about parenting as an adoptive mother is the opportunity to help my child grow into a caring, thoughtful, smart, and hilariously funny young lady. I love watching with amazement and encouragement as she uses her natural talents in musical theater and competitive swimming.

87. Kotane, age 57.

The unparalleled stuff in parenting is partnering with God and pouring unconditional love into your children. It's tilling the soil and watching your kids grow and seeing the fruit of your labor of love. It's following God's ways, prospering in His faithfulness, and continuing the legacy.

88. Nan, age 42.

The prize in parenting is being able to pay tribute to my parents. It is the diversity of the loving community established to support, encourage, and guide your child because it does indeed take a village.

But in just one sentence, the greatest part of parenting is seeing life shape kids through God's hands.

89. Ray, age 44, five children.

As a father of a son with special needs, I think the best part of parenting is when kids give love back to you. That might be different for me, but I feel this especially with my son with autism who has trouble communicating.

90. John, age 30.

The most fulfilling part of parenting is watching and helping my son grow and develop. It is standing back and watching him take on different challenges and persevere through them.

91. Lemoil, age 46.

The joy in being a parent is watching your children grow and being present in their lives.

92. Pat, age 61.

Fine parenting is the satisfaction of raising good people who contribute to society.

93. Drew, age 53, one daughter.

The elation parenting brings is that you come to the realization that all of the stuff that you were missing before you had children disappear when they are born. They fill all your voids. Parenting is life-changing.

94. Rick, age 67, two adult children.

The most satisfying part about parenting is seeing your kids do well at something. It's when things finally connect and you see them going in the right direction to identify and reach their full potential.

95. Leonard, age 63, six adult children.

The best part of parenting is building my children's strength to handle the ugly and hurtful situations in the world with gratefulness and contentment, trusting the power within. I trust that doing this will saturate them with a peace that transcends all understanding and give them everlasting joy. Parenting is the gift that teaches me what is important in life, and that is love. This is not an easy lesson.

96. Trimbra, age 64.

The most heart-felt part of parenting is that I get to be a world-changer. My children will ultimately change the picture of the world. I want them to be lovely inside and out to add beauty to the portrait. When I get exhausted I shake myself back into focus and delight in receiving and giving the authentic love that continuously bubbles between parent and child.

97. Christopher, age 43.

My takeaway from being a parent is that it reminds you to be a child again.

98. Ivan, age 68, four adult children.

The coolest part of parenting is raising another human being. It's protecting them because, honestly, we don't live in a kind world. You will always be a parent. And as a parent you never stop striving to help shape your child's life into something that matters in this world.

99. Michelle, age 31.
The maximum compensation of parenting is that children give you purpose. This allows you to learn to be selfless.

100. Kendra, age 43.
The part of parenting that makes me want to spring out of bed is that I continually learn, and this strengthens my faith. Parenting helps me to understand in a more profound way the relationship that I have with God by seeing it through my relationship with my children. It doesn't deliver instant rewards but rather an everlasting love.

101. Joni, age 75.
The snuggles are the cherries of parenting, especially at bedtime.

102. Jessica, age 69.
I love being a parent, and you are a parent for the rest of your life no matter how old you grow or how old your children are.

103. Melissa, age 40.
The most gleeful times of parenting are when I am able to spend time with my daughter and listen to her. I am recent-

ly divorced and have to share time with her father. The hardest part of the divorce is not seeing my daughter every day like I used to. I cherish our time together. She makes my heart sing.

104. Arthur, age 43, two daughters.

    The supreme element of parenting is everything, the highs and the lows.

105. Diana, age 35.

    Seeing my daughter develop in all areas of her life and the unlimited love that I exchange with her is the most pleasing part of parenting.

106. Marine, age 38.

    The richness of parenting is that it's done through unrestricted and total love.

107. Tom, age 45.

    I appreciate the days when my kids do what I request of them when I ask them. It's even better if they do it before I have to remind them because they know it needs to be done. This is my sign that they are growing up and making responsible choices. That is irrefutably the most precious gift of parenting.

It is worth every struggle that you face as a parent to be called *blessed*.

> *Her children arise and call her blessed;*
> *her husband also, and he praises her:*
> Proverbs 31:28 (NIV)

The father of the righteous will greatly rejoice, And he who sires a wise son will be glad in him.

Proverbs 23:24 (ESV)

I hope that you gained a few new ideas about parenting from reading this book. If you noticed areas where you wish that you had done things differently, don't be too hard on yourself. Today is the day to make adjustments.

> *When you know better you do better.*
> — Maya Angelou

I love Ms. Angelou's quote.

Don't beat yourself up, but *do* make changes immediately, and do what you have now learned is better. It is never too late to do better. If you have teenagers, adult children, or grandchildren, start now.

When God reveals shortcomings to me now, I still apologize to my adult children for things that I could have done better. A close friend relates it this way: *If God reveals it, it is for Him to heal it.* This allows you to amend your wrong and for God to heal those you hurt.

When you feel like you have done your best and you can't do more, relinquish control and trust God. These words are voiced often, but I find it exceedingly challenging to live by them when chaos breaks out. I remind myself as I weep and I'm paralyzed with complete defeat to re-focus and pray.

So I encourage you, don't forget to pray your way to the sweetness of a loving God. God is faithful!

About the Author

Tonya Milligan is a Denver-based speaker and small business owner. Using her 30 years of experience as a child enrichment director, she founded the company *Rent-A-Theme Entertainment,* bringing learning through the joy of play to schools and child care centers throughout the Denver Metro area.

Tonya writes with passion, knowledge, and wisdom. Her life experience working with thousands of parents and children has helped her develop a system to cultivate and nourish children toward achieving their full potential.

"Often the informational books I encounter spend a majority of the text trying to convince you why their method is important and then offering general principles with occasional examples. However, they don't offer a systematic approach on how to implement what the author is advocating. Mom's book, on the other hand, not only offers tips but provides a system by which you can become a better parent and does so while providing engaging anecdotes that help illustrate the points along the way."

—Dr. Kenneth K Milligan

www.ingramcontent.com/pod-product-compliance
Lightning Source LLC
Chambersburg PA
CBHW050151130526
44591CB00033B/1249